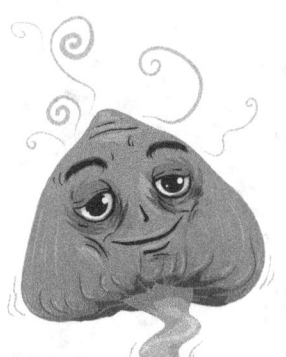

Psychedelic Art

Psychedelic came from the word "Psychedelos" which means open the spirit. Psychedelic art is a type of visual expression of the inner world and can be form in Optical illusion, Distorted Image, Fractals, Melting, Symmetry, Glitches and Deep Dream Also, in Numeric art, Street art or architecture. The climax of the psychedelic art was peaked in the '60s, arguing for an open mind and consciousness for global peace and solutions in the society.

Instructions (Not mandatory)

- Use bright colors (Eg: Middle Yellow, Vivid Red, Malachite, Shocking Pink, Interdimensional Blue and Turquoise Blue).
- Try not to miss the glitch and distortion whether its appropriate.
- Paint/Color it yourself and dont complain!

Your thoughts are seeds
Brain is the garden
Acid is the Fertilizer
Take the trip and flourish

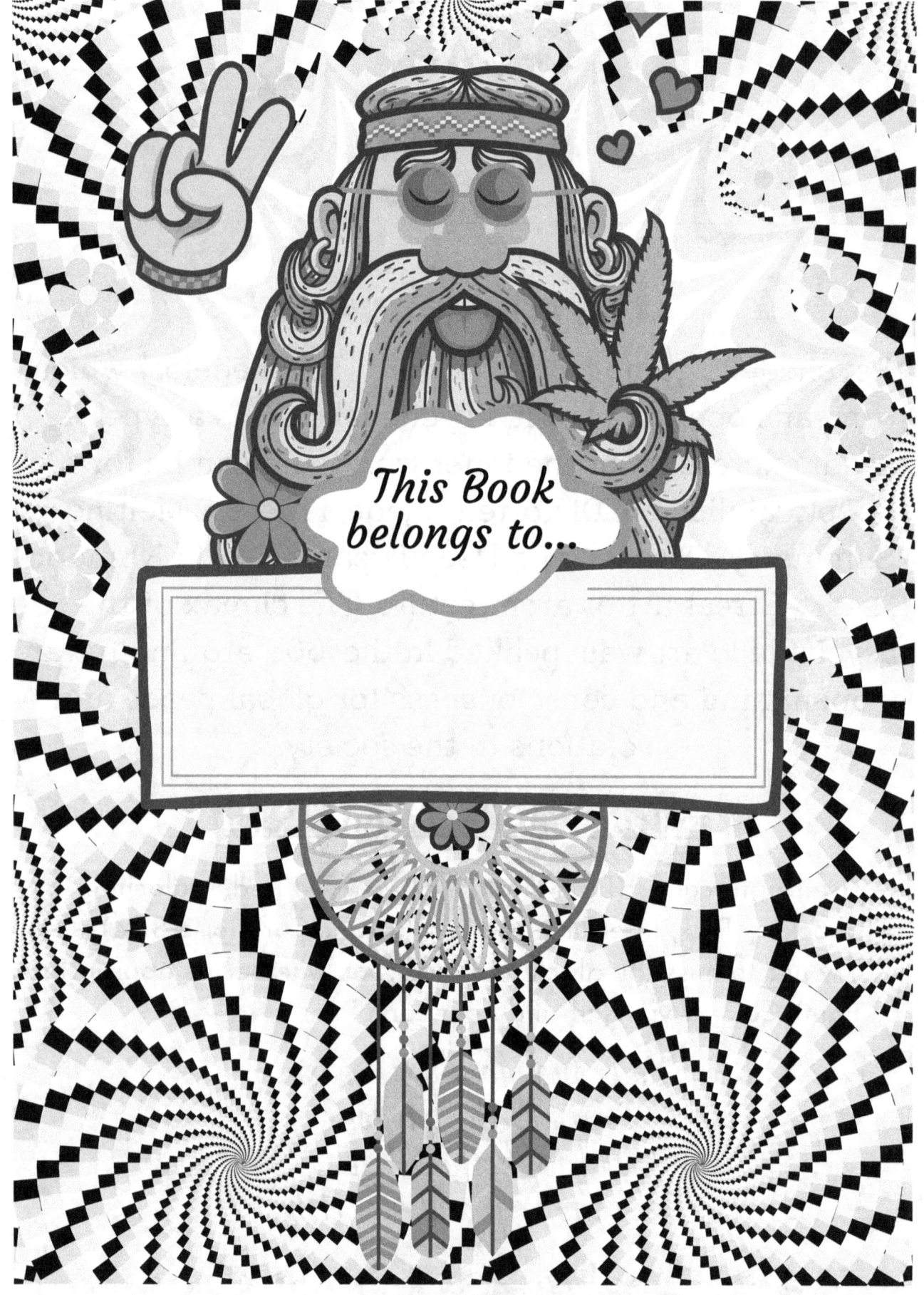

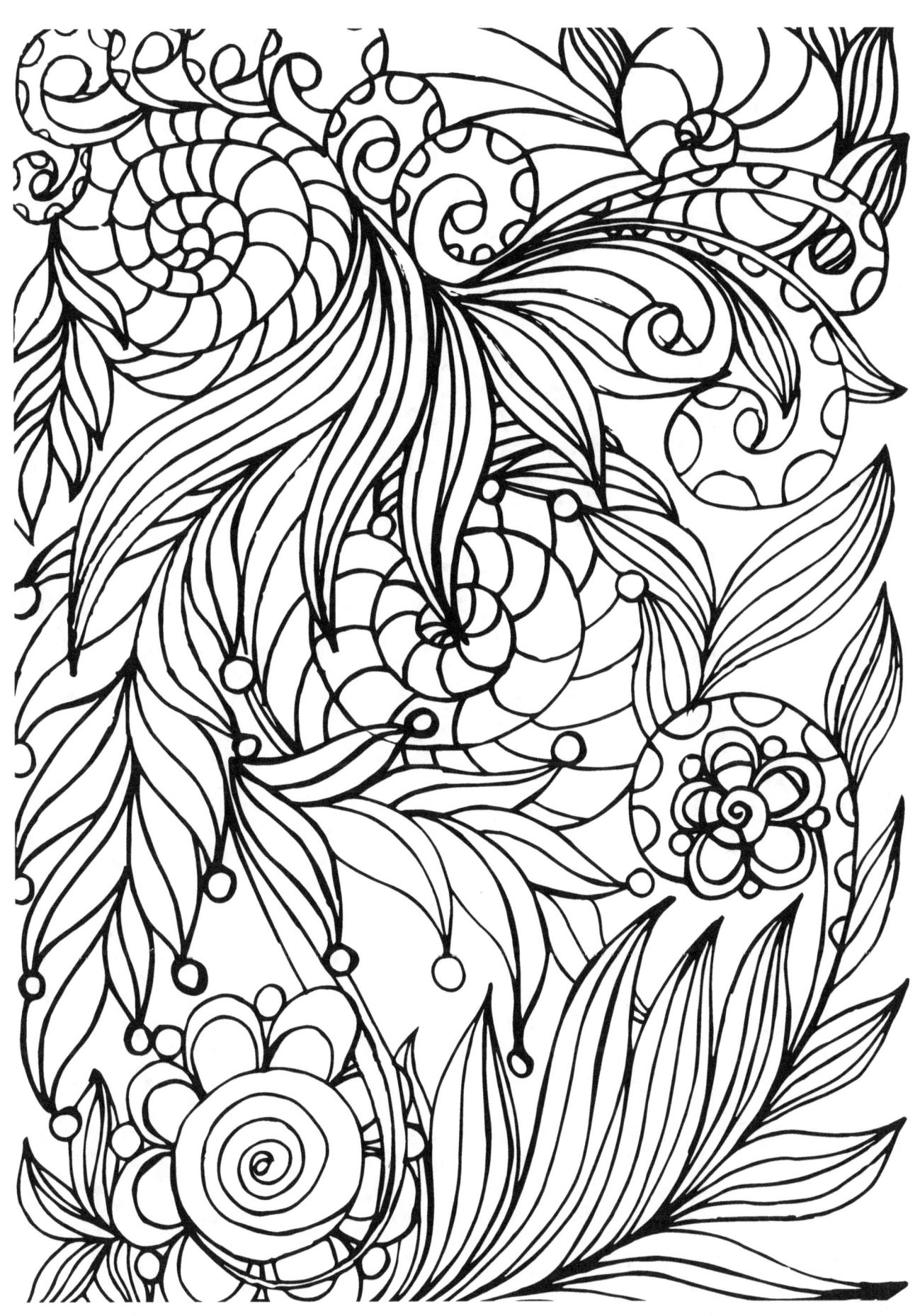

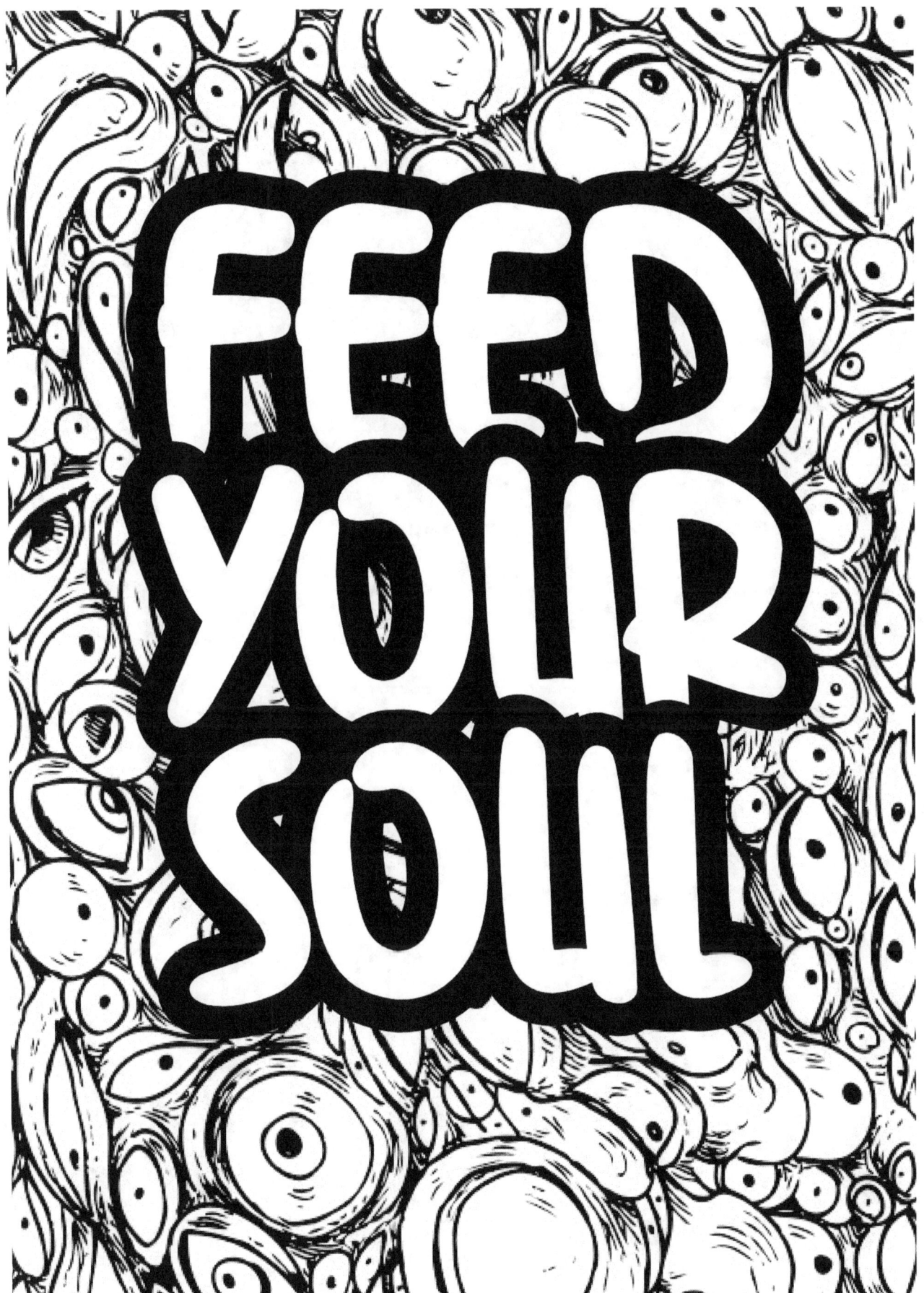

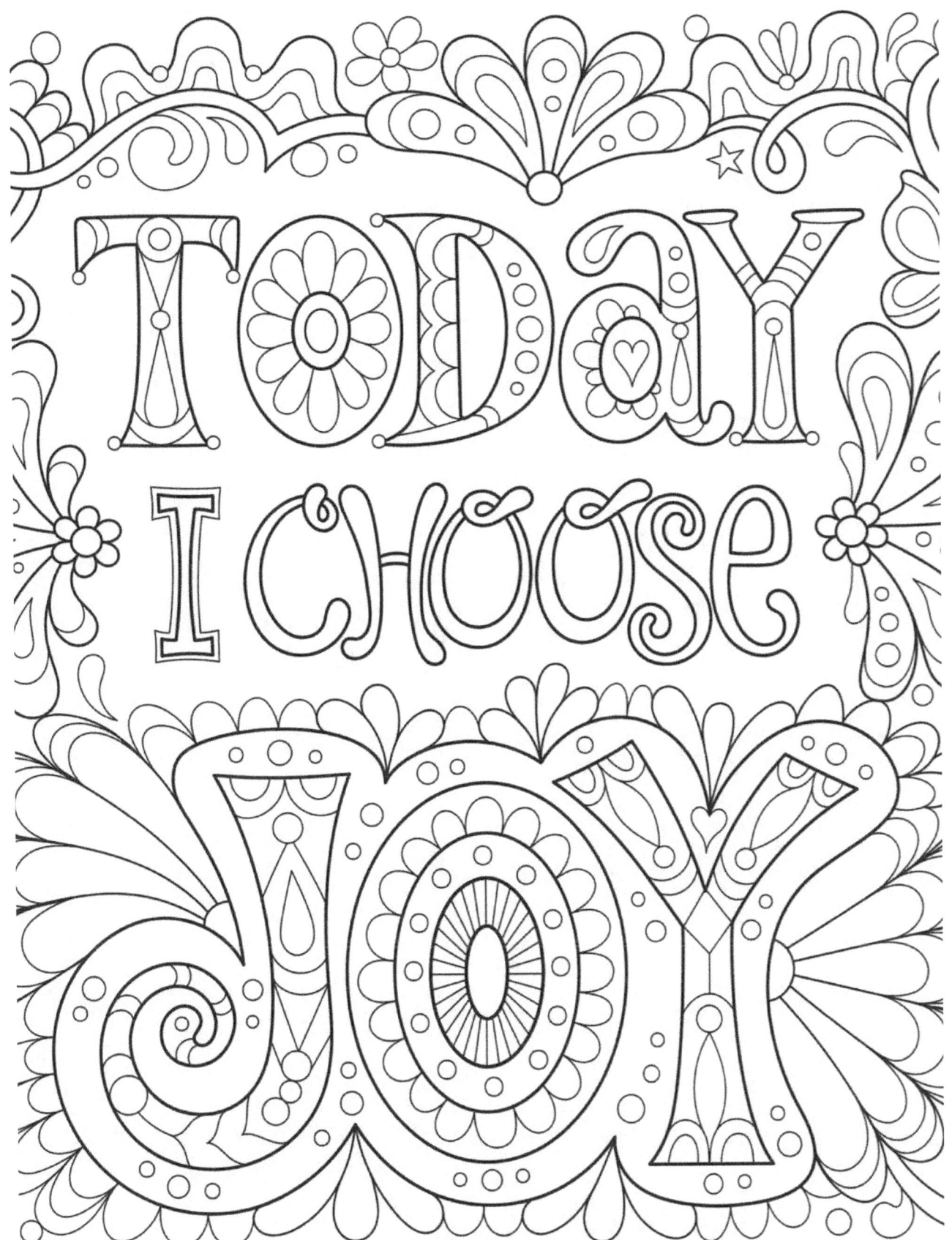

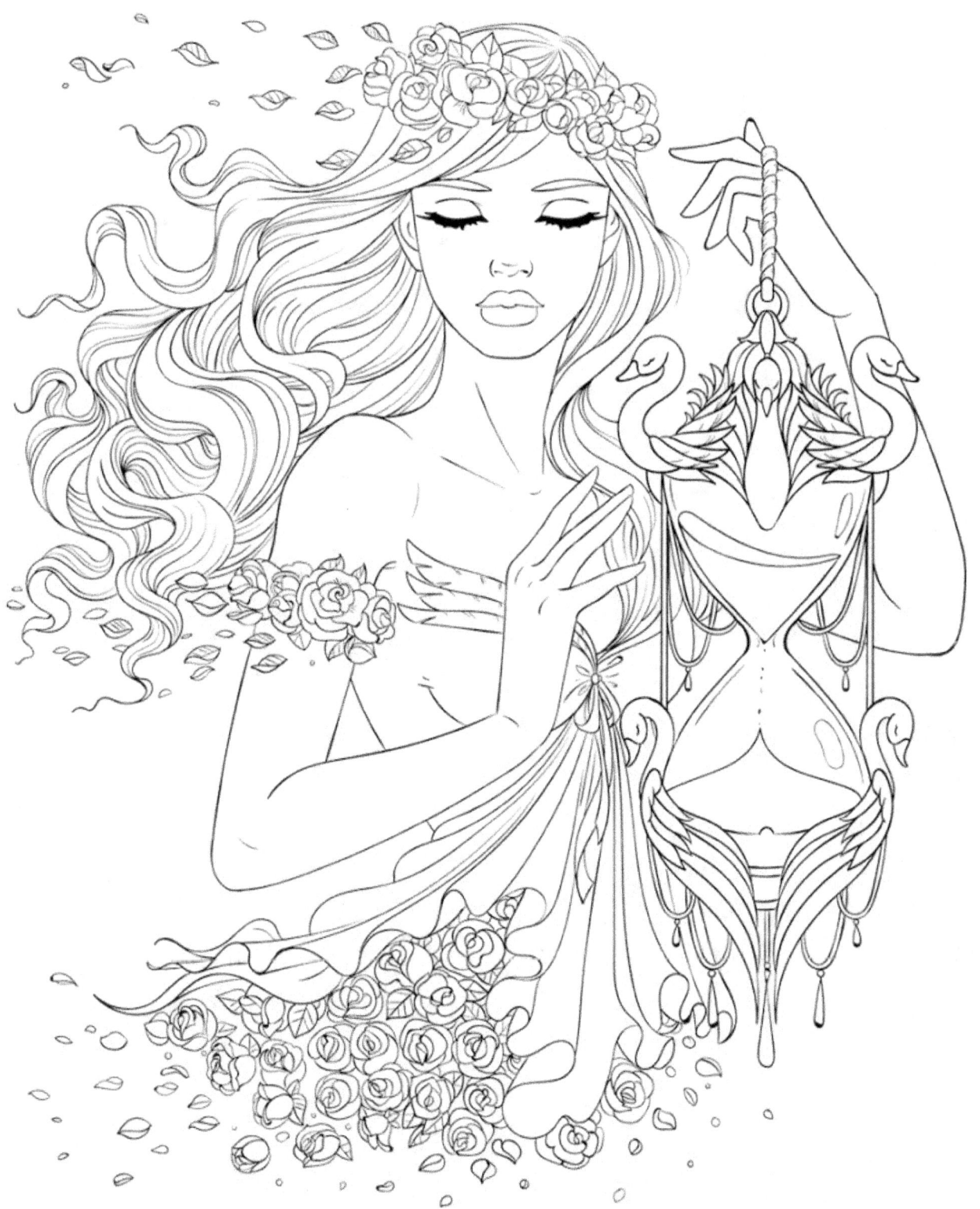

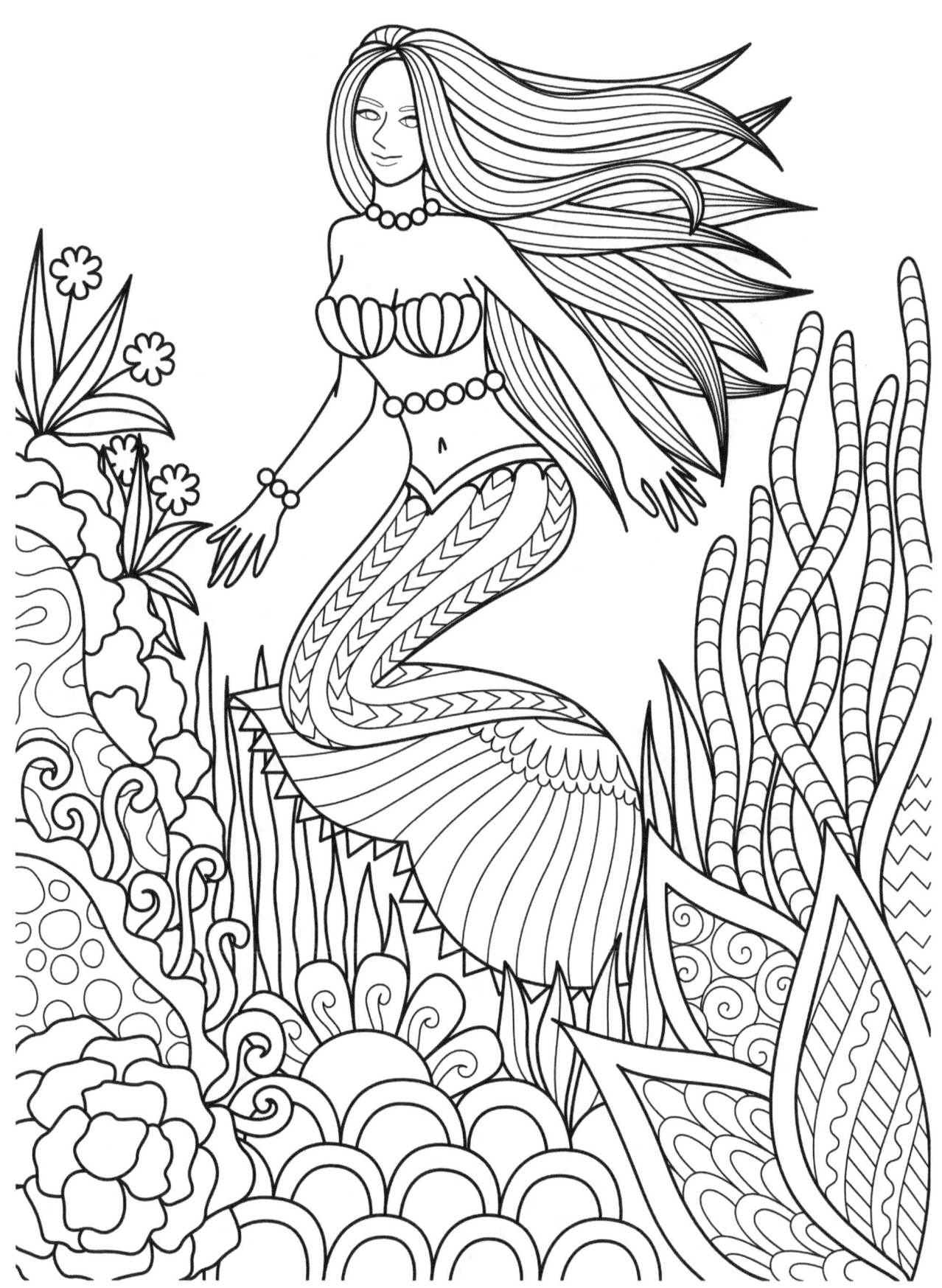

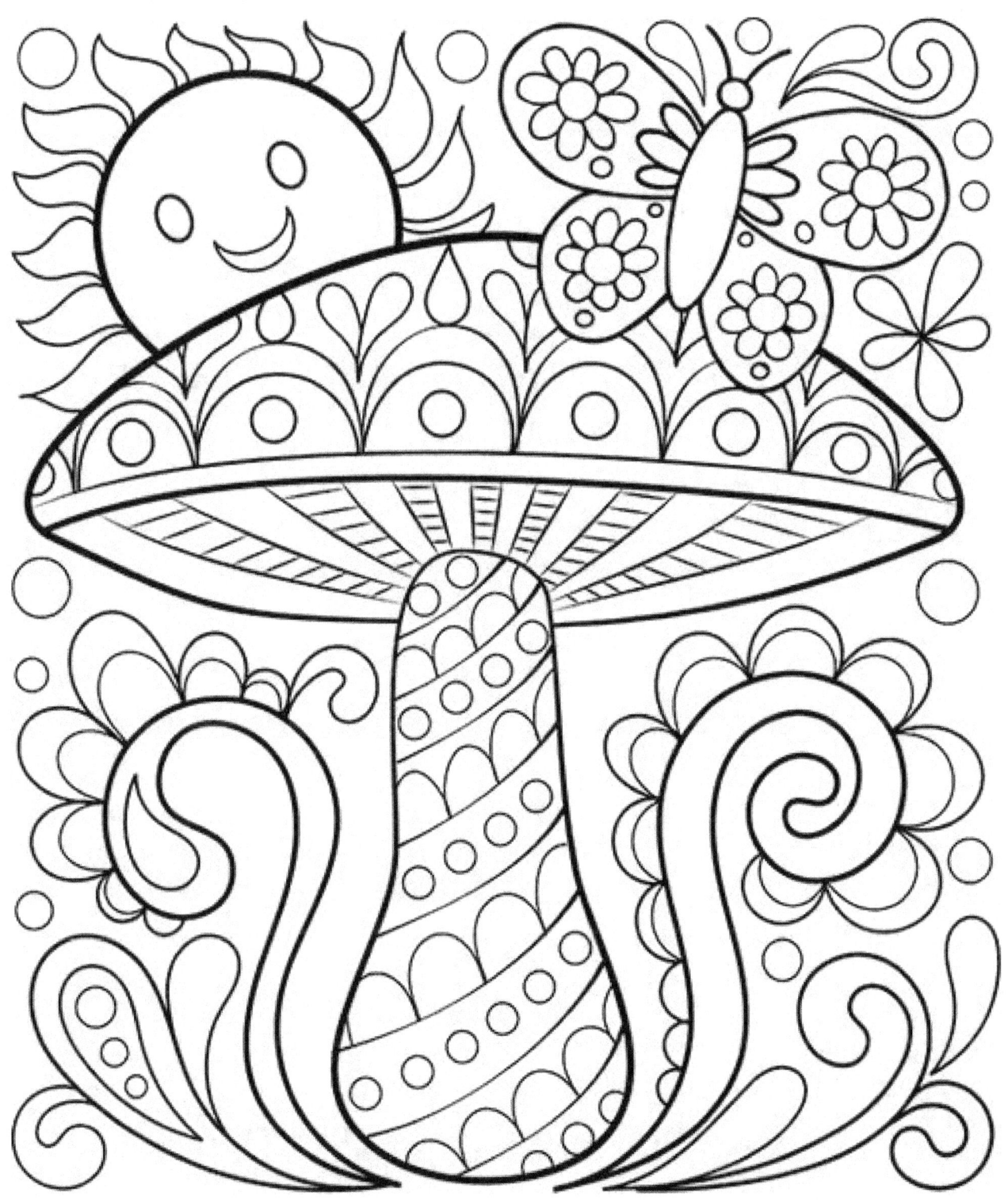

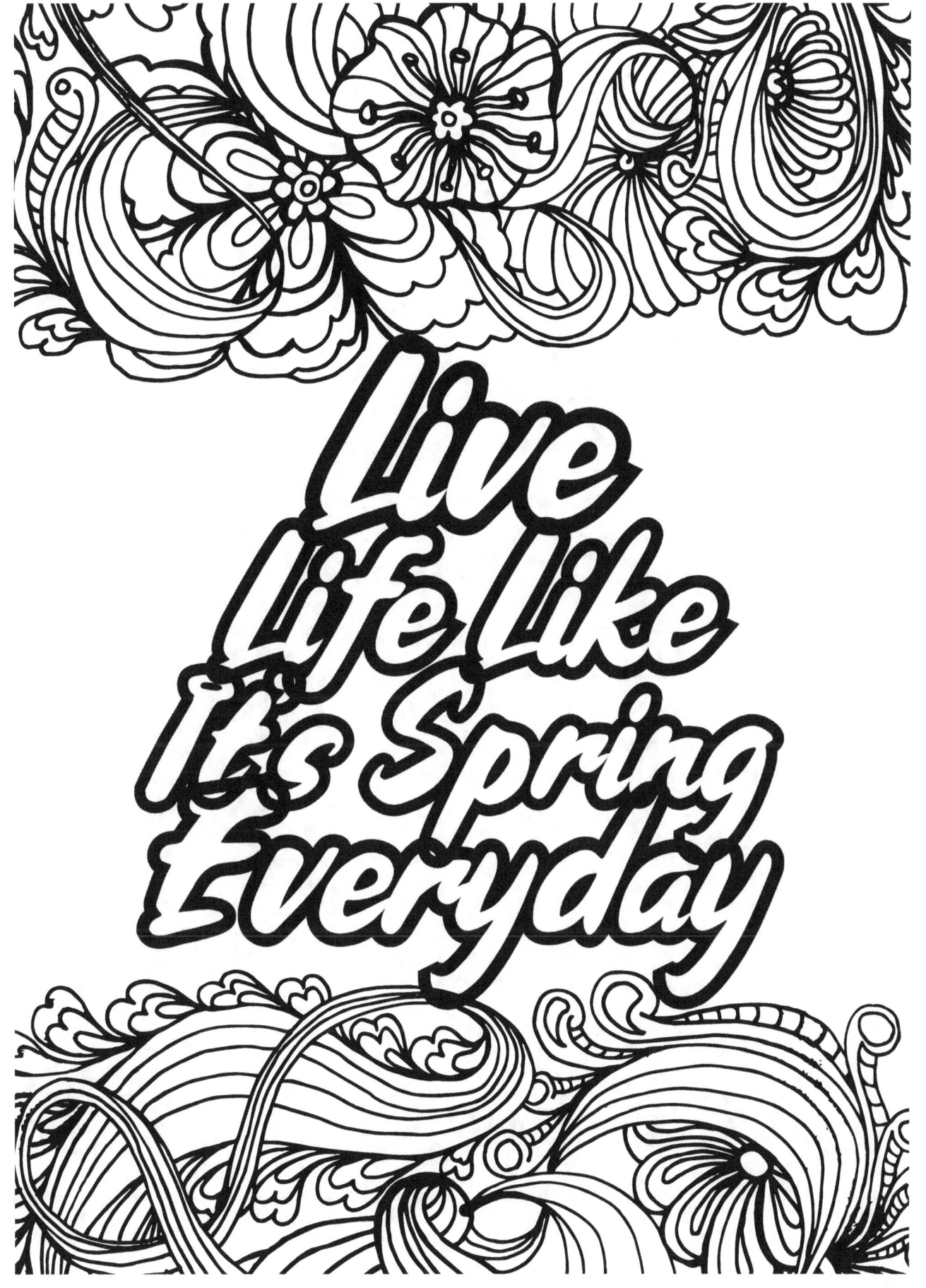

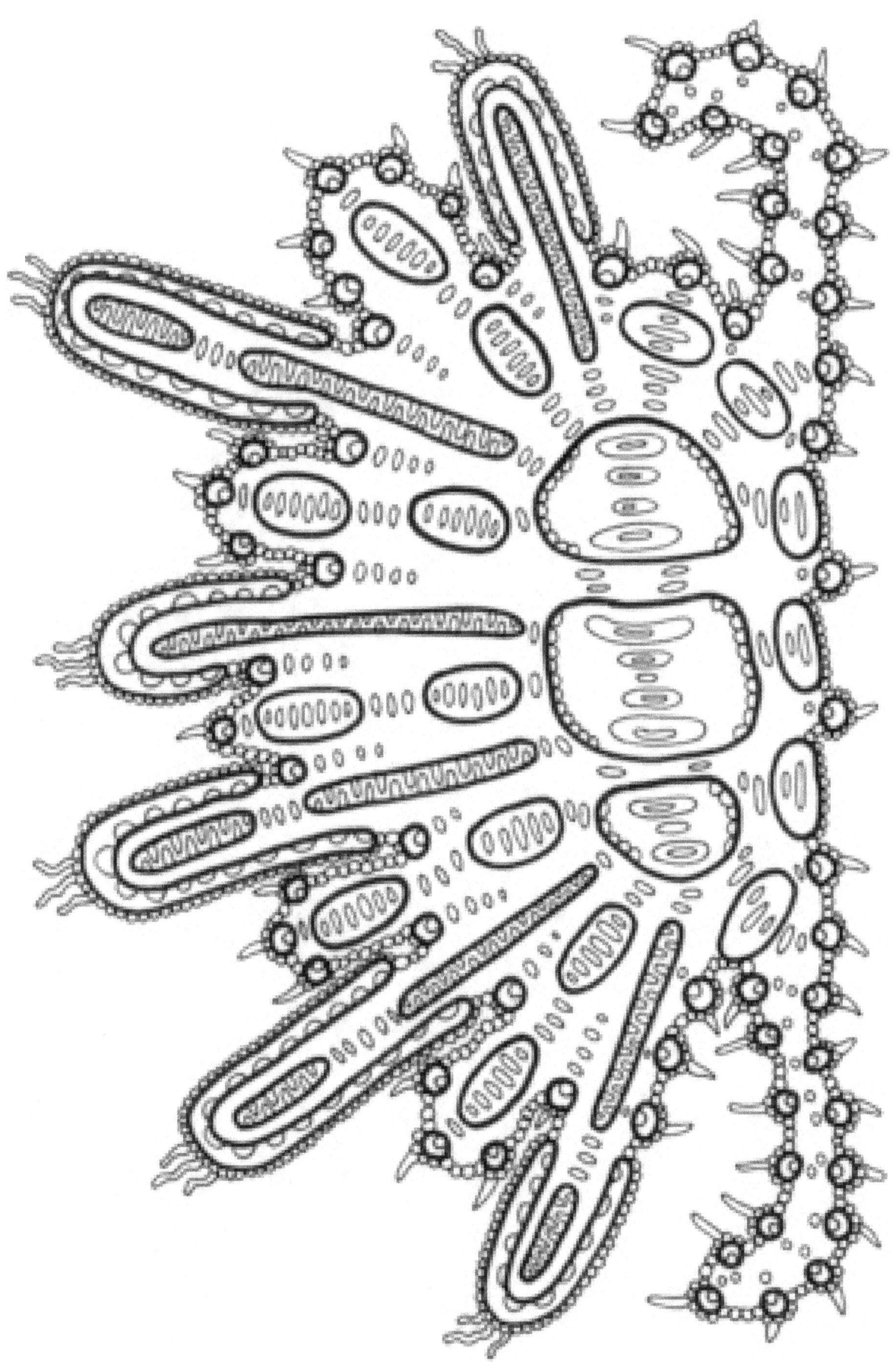

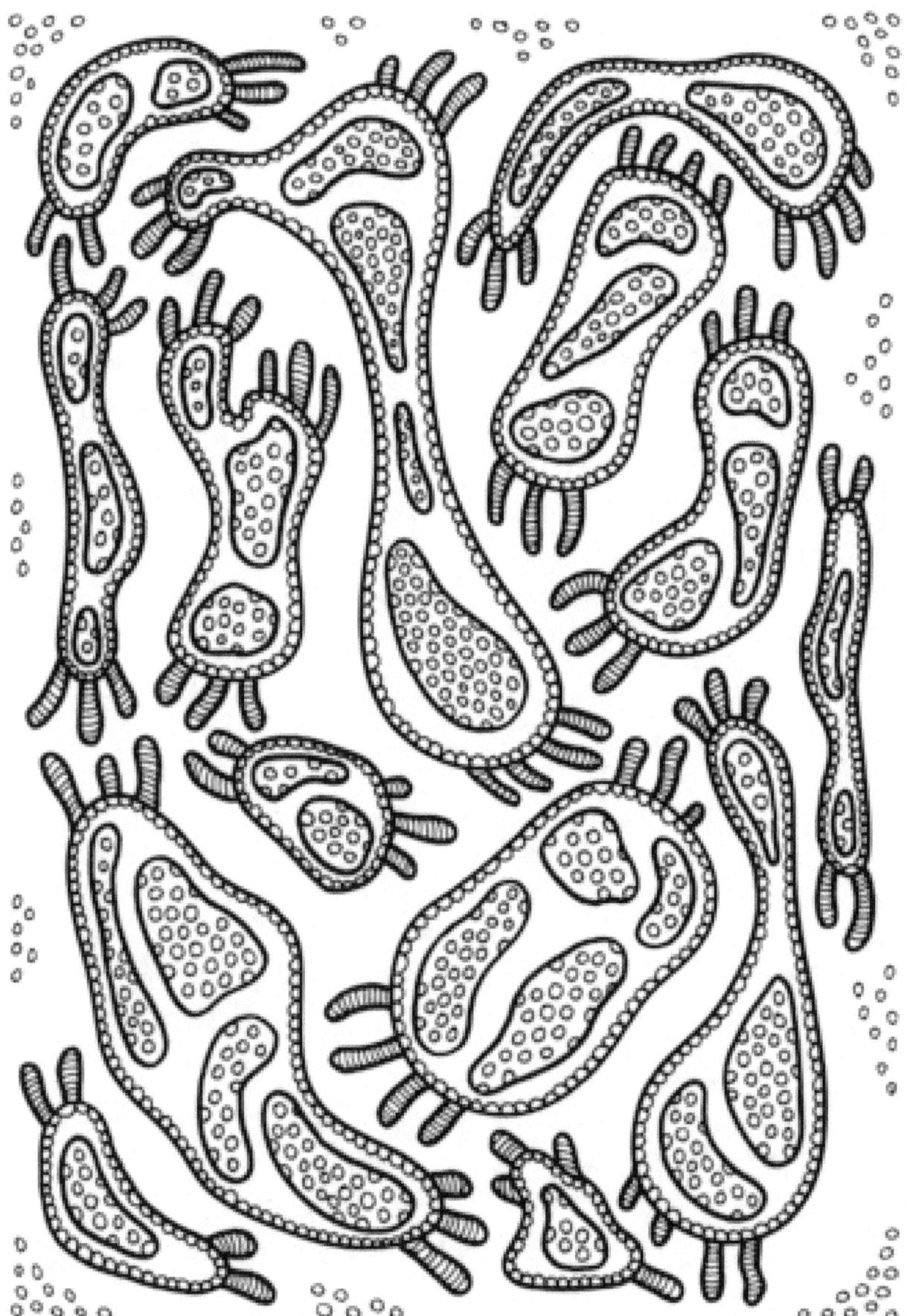

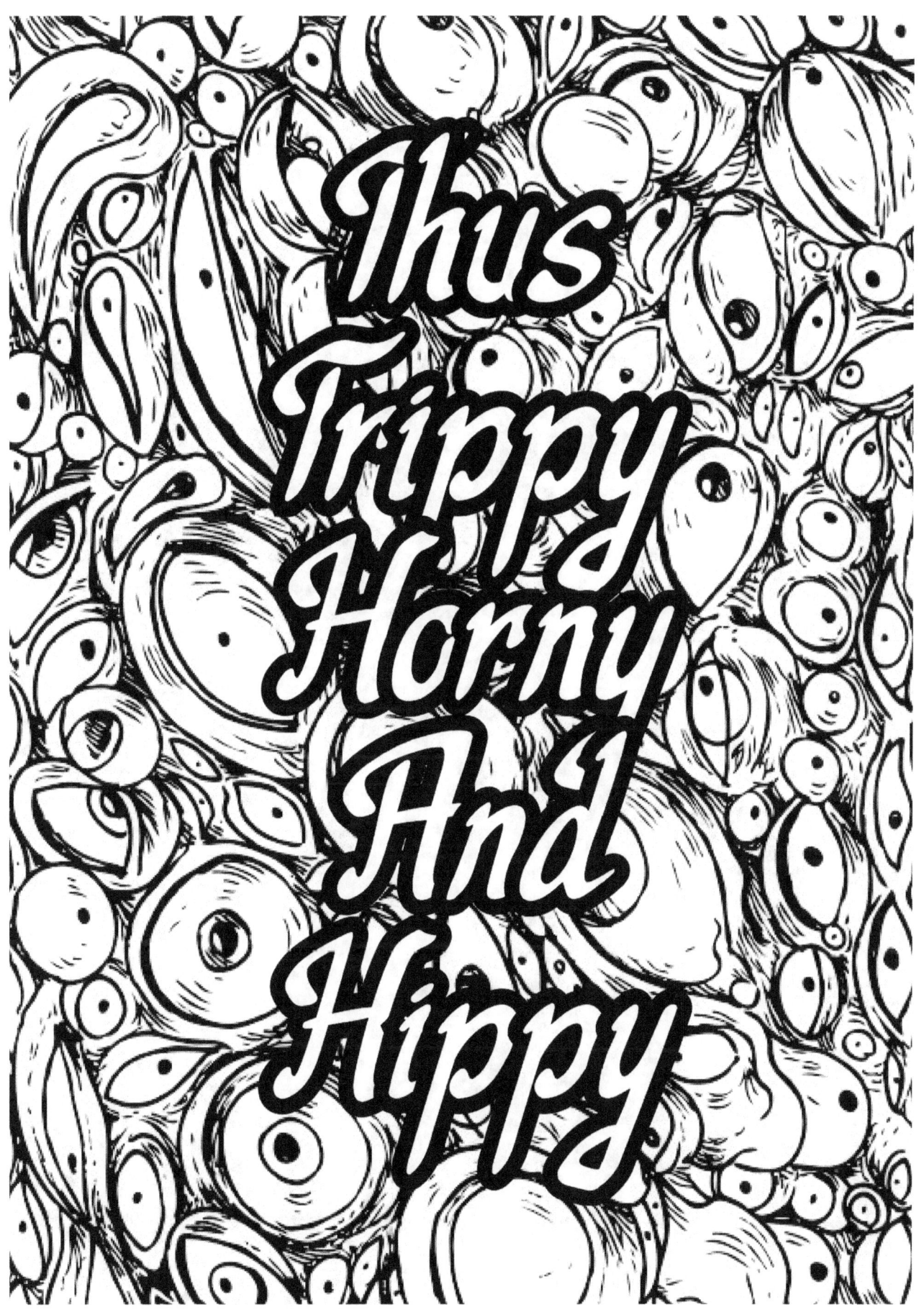

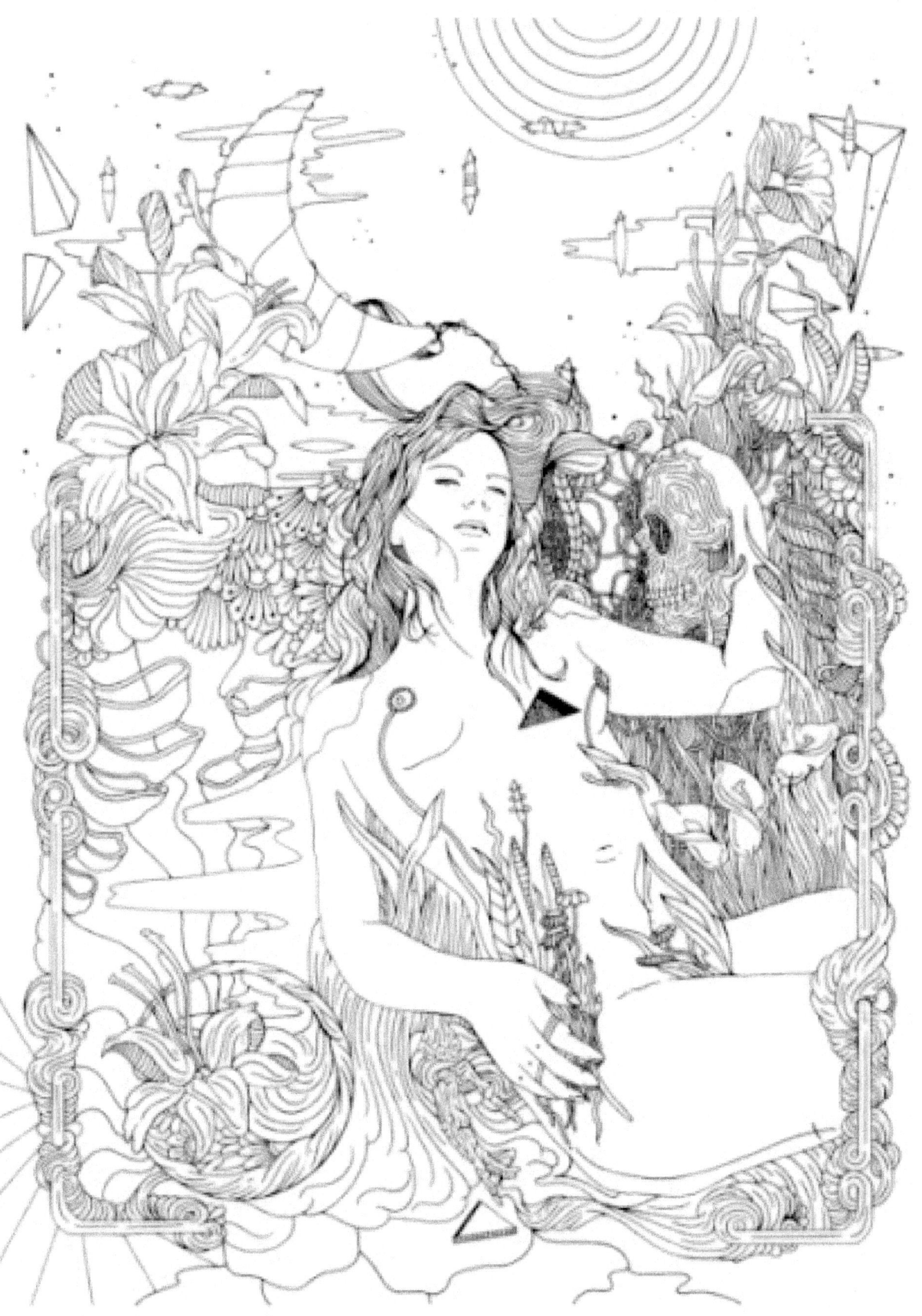

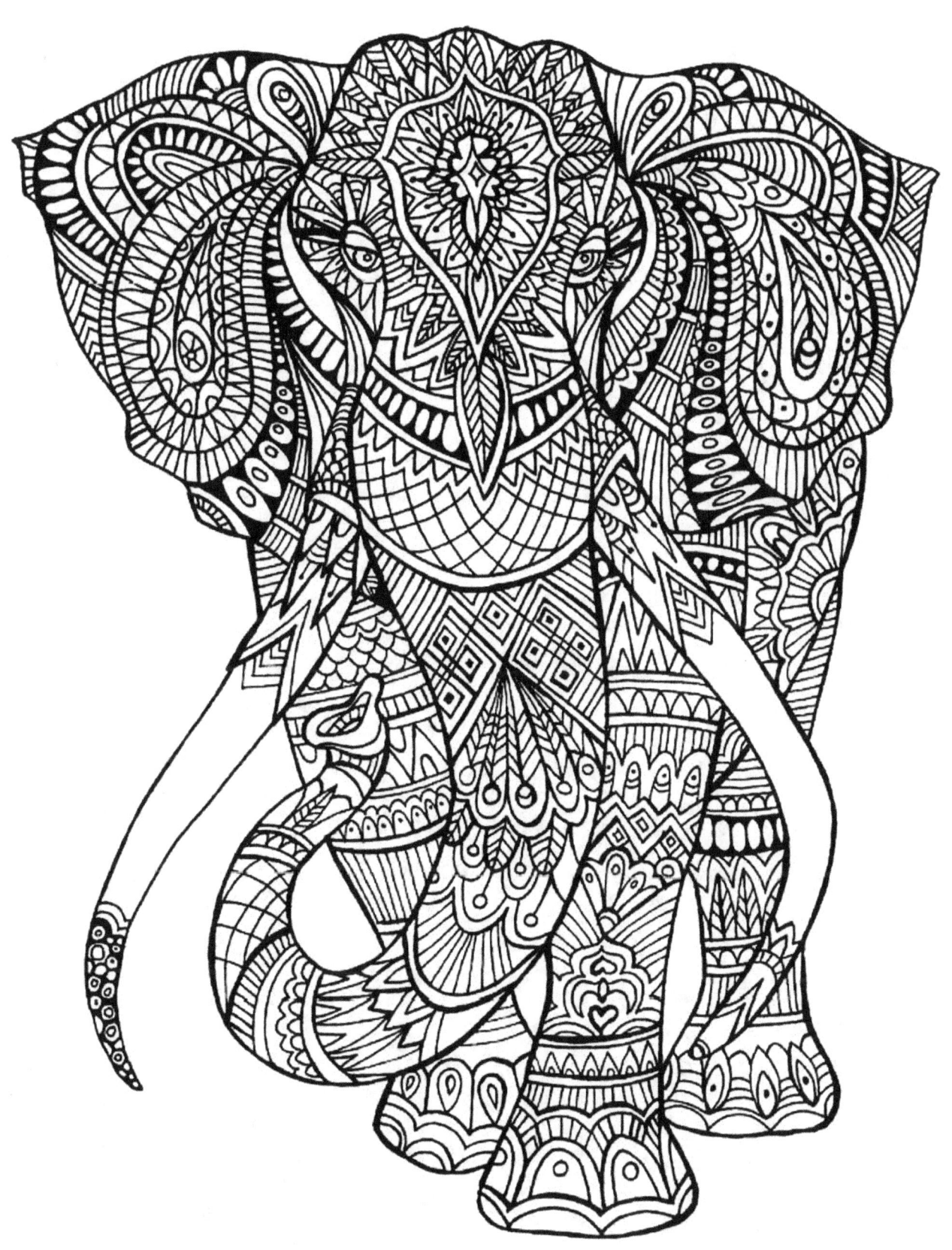

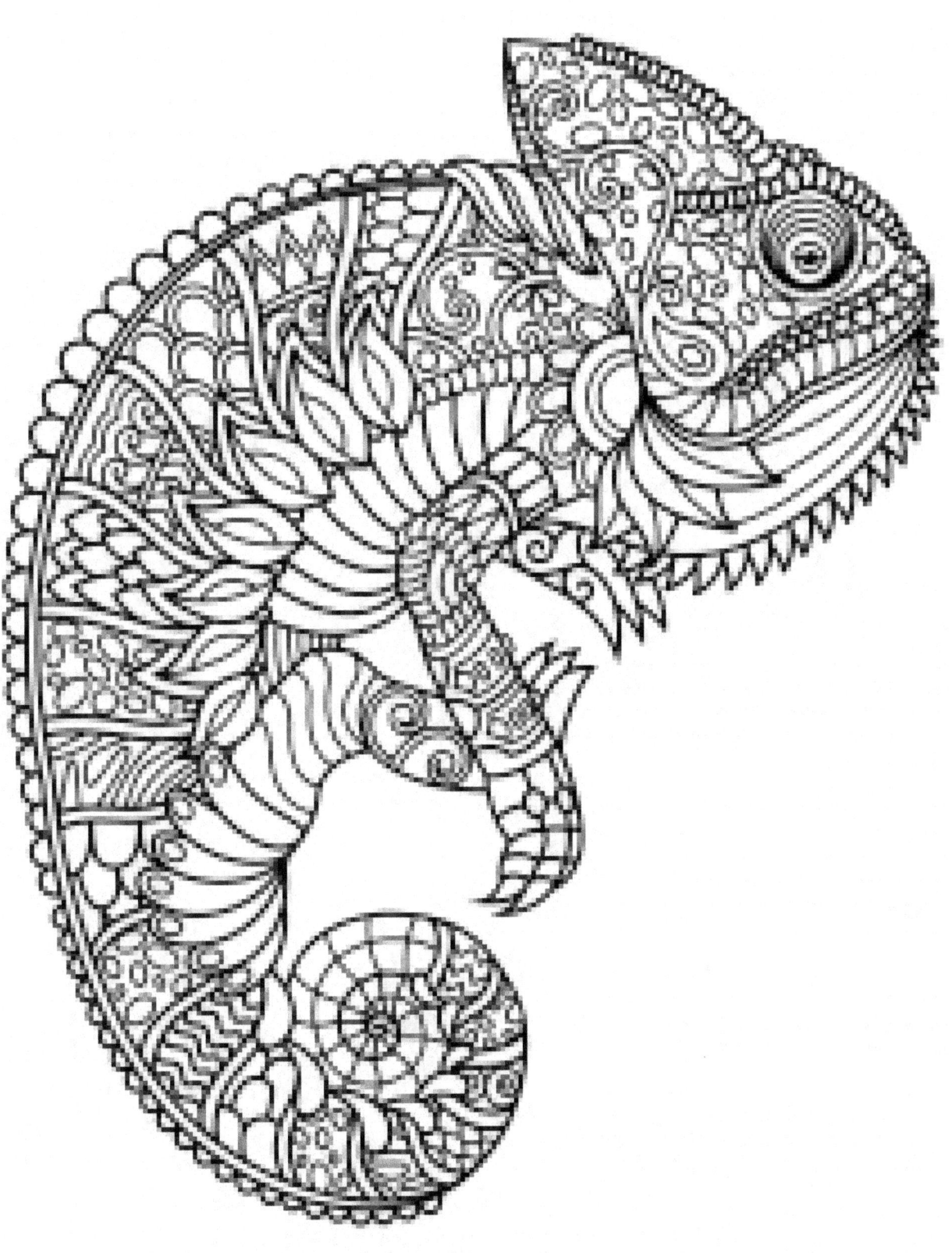

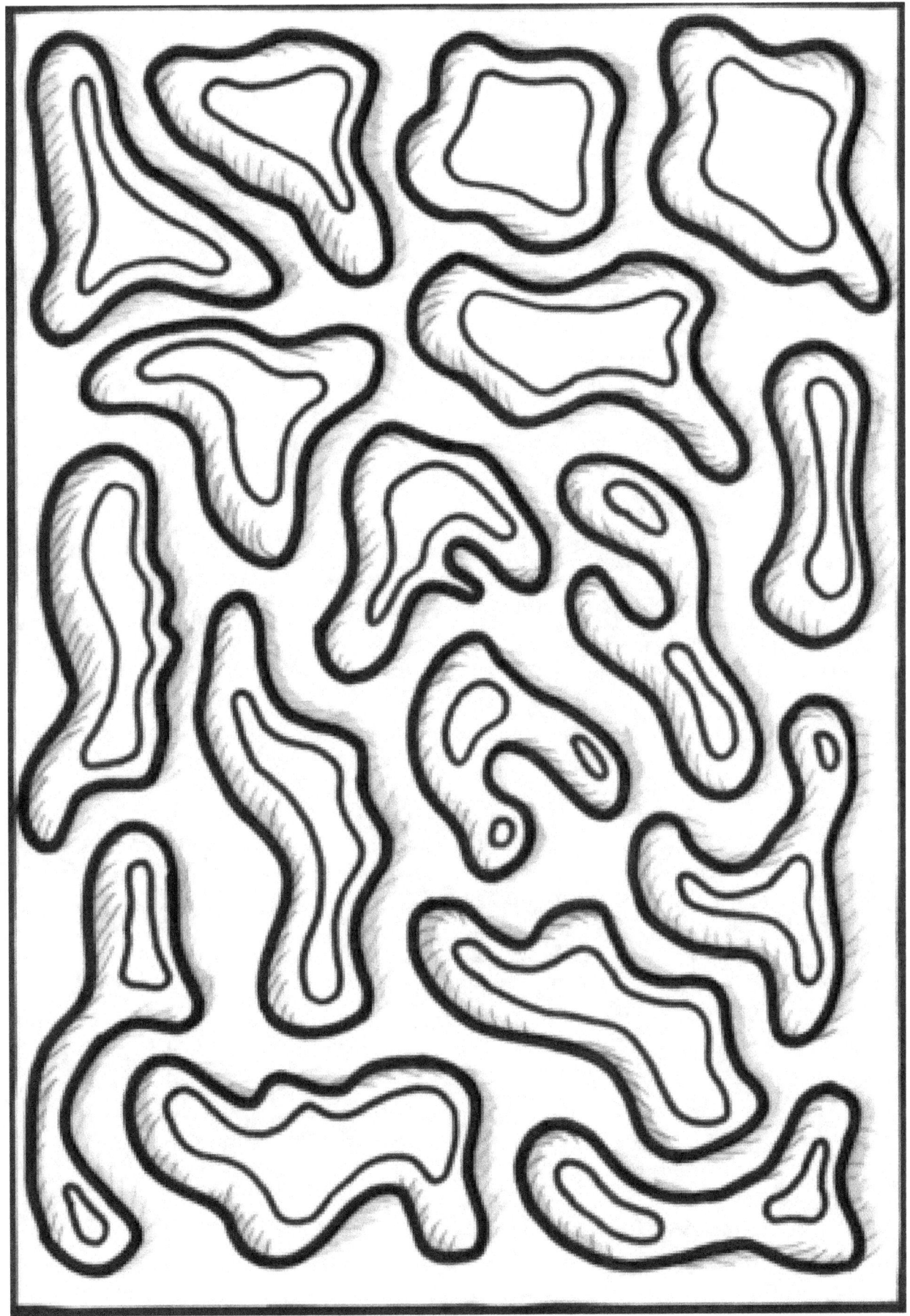

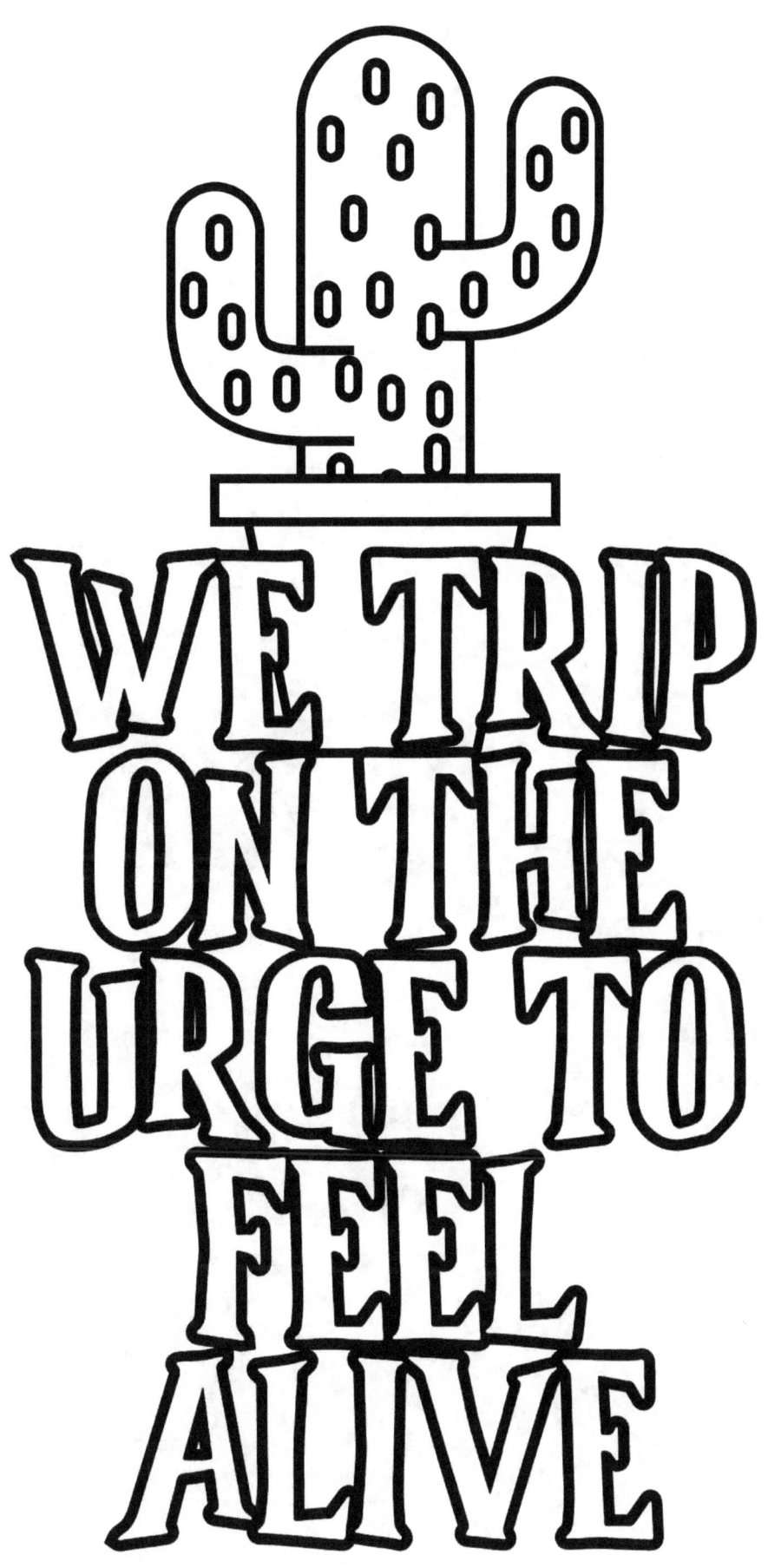

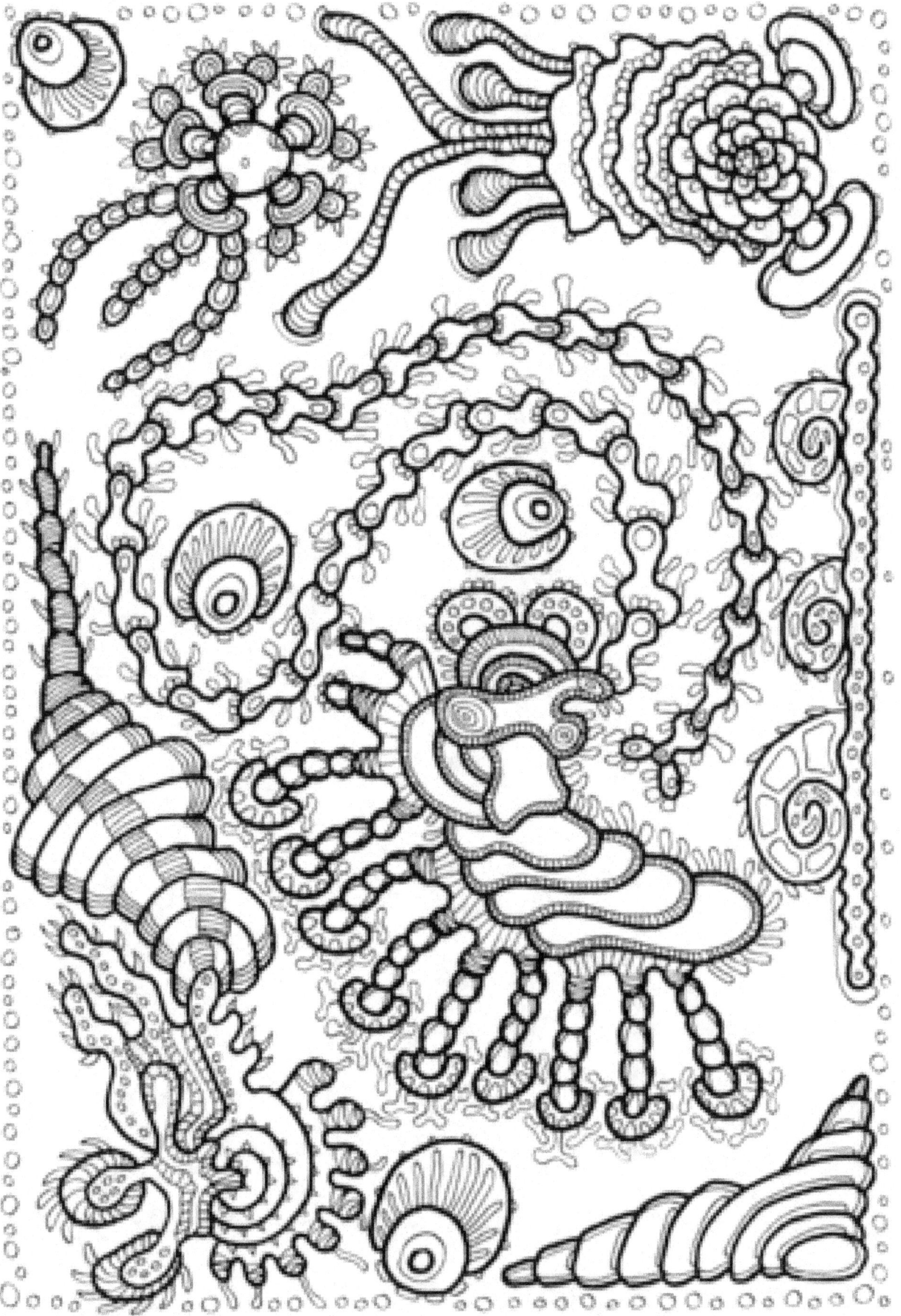

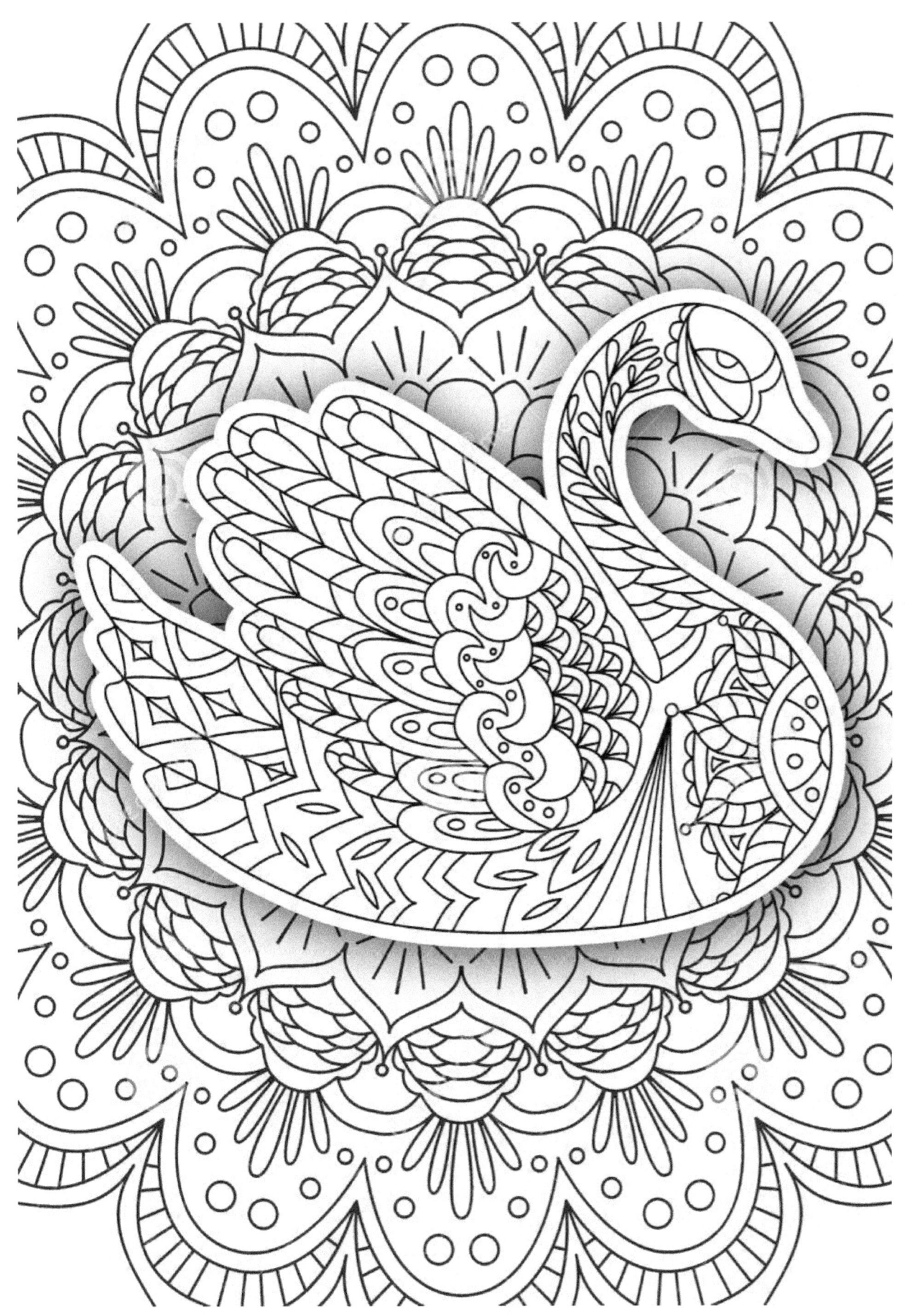

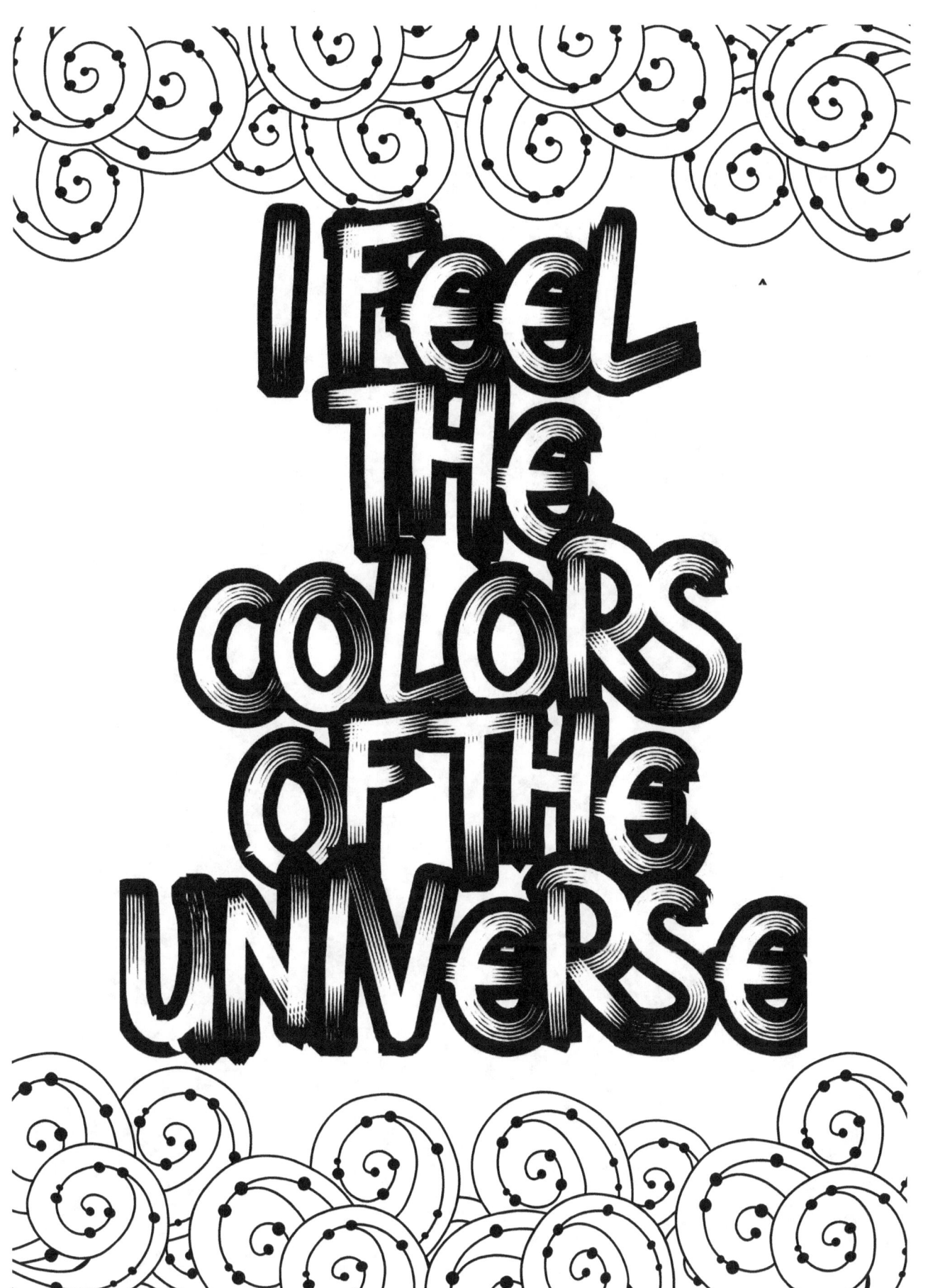

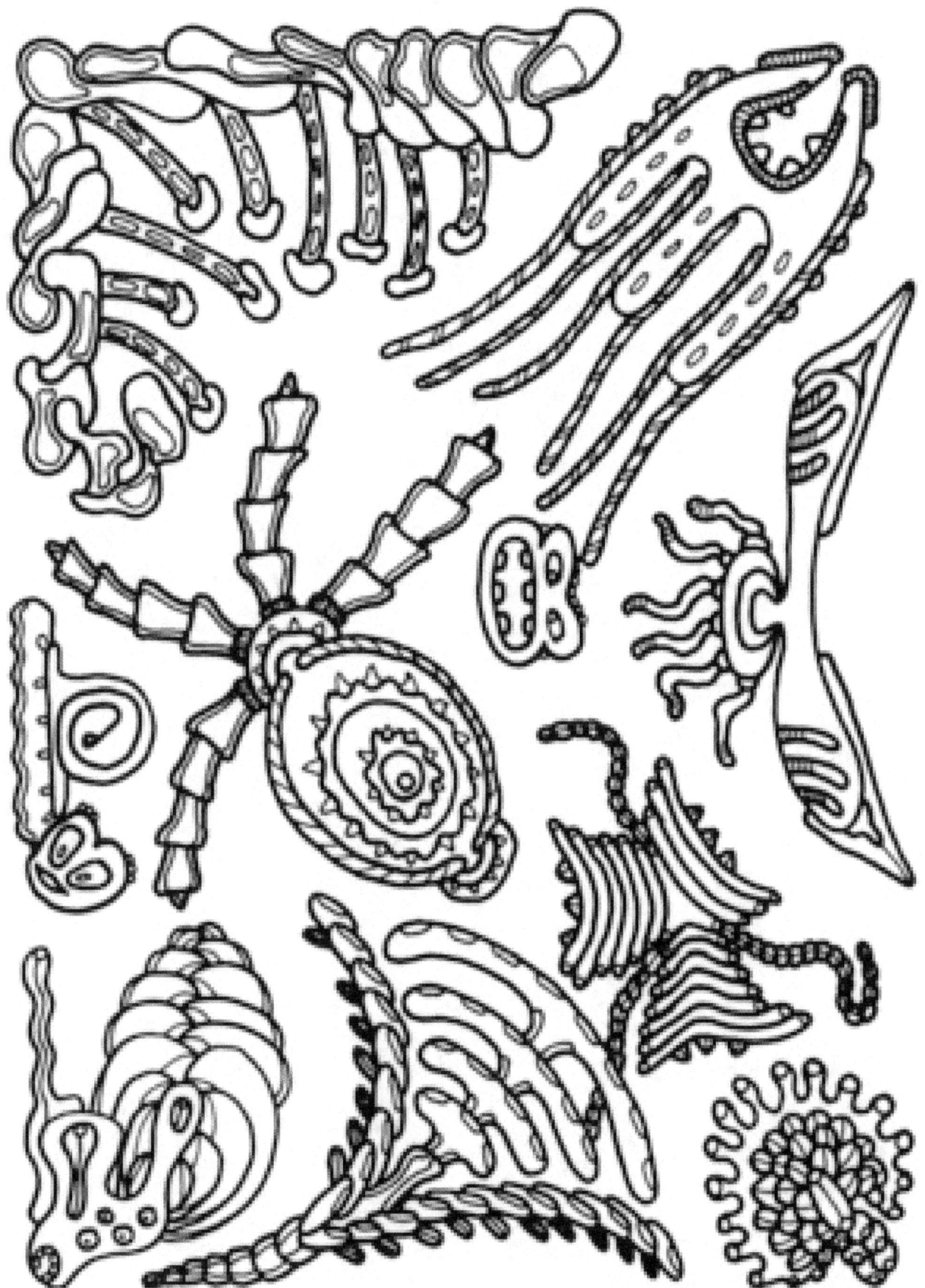

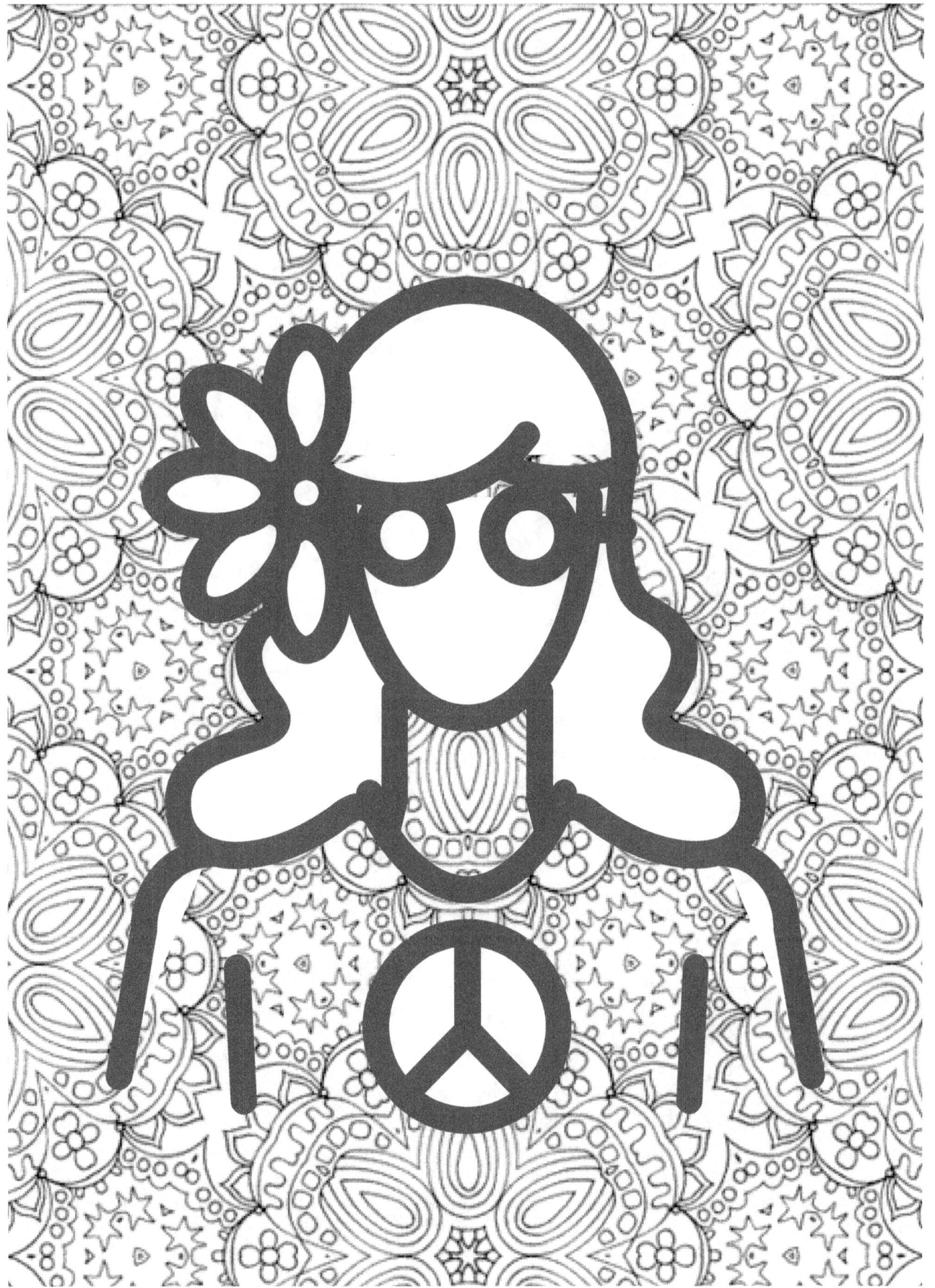

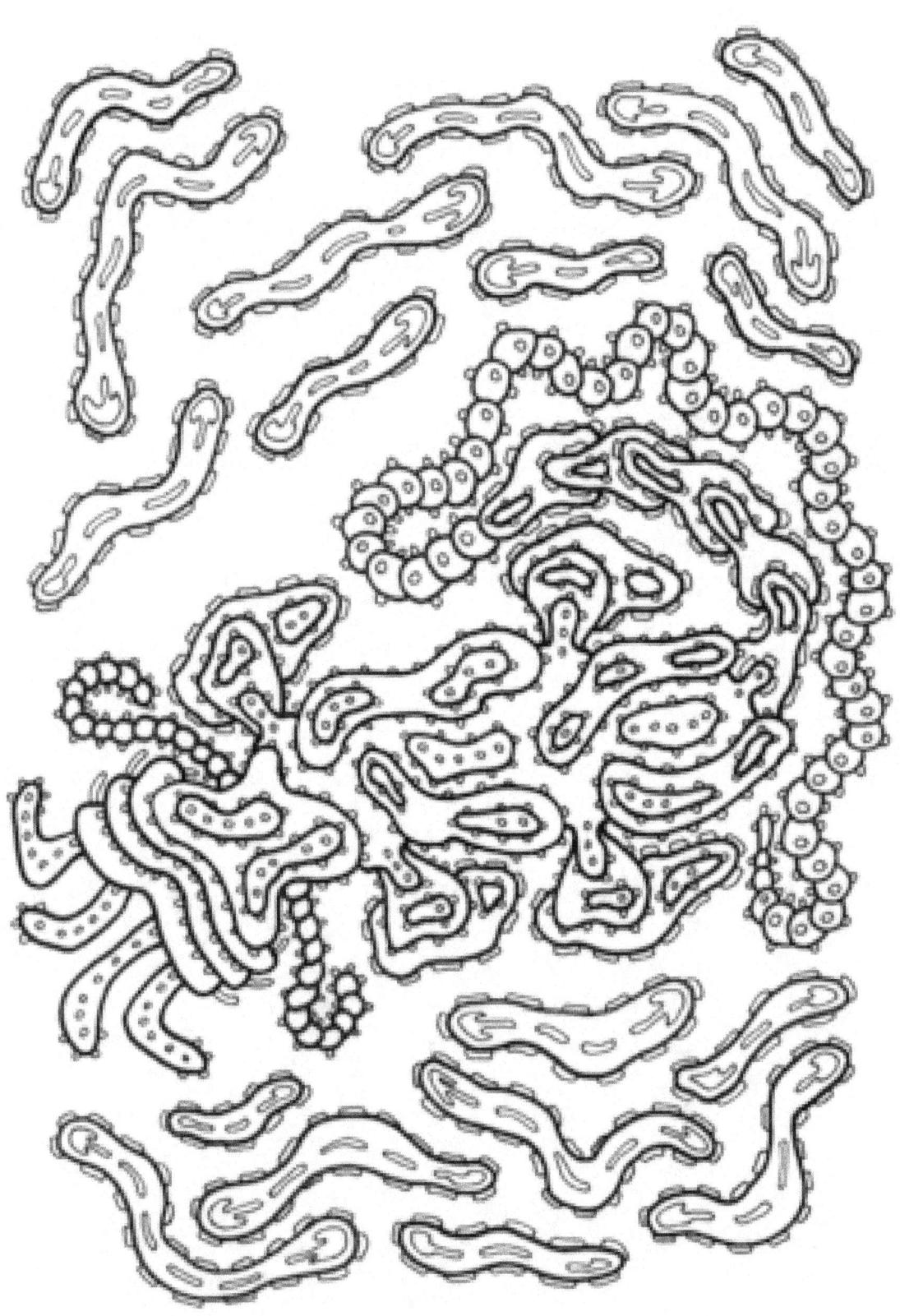

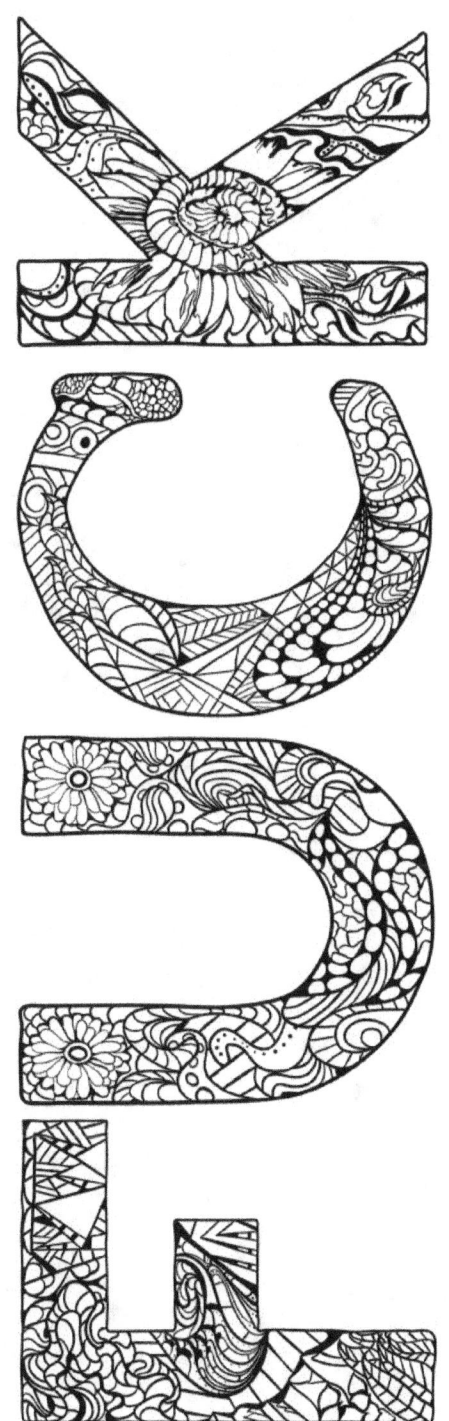
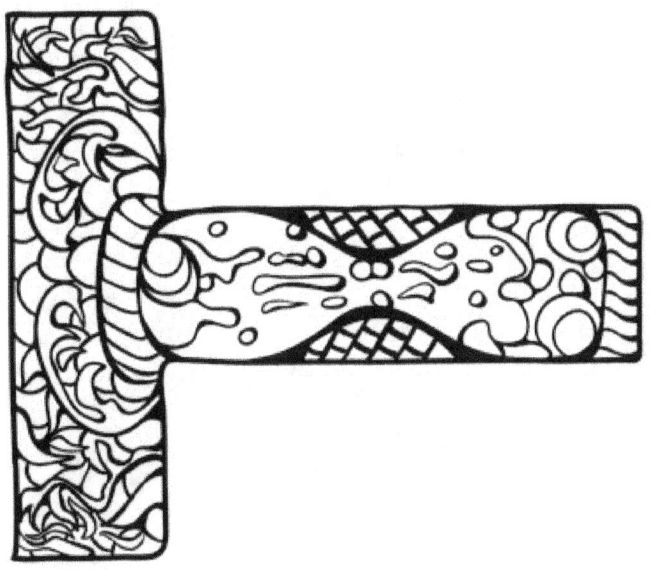
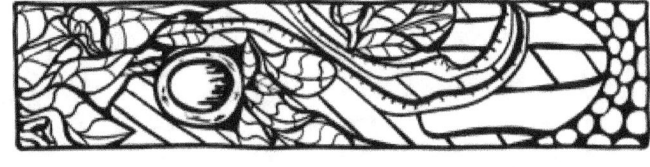

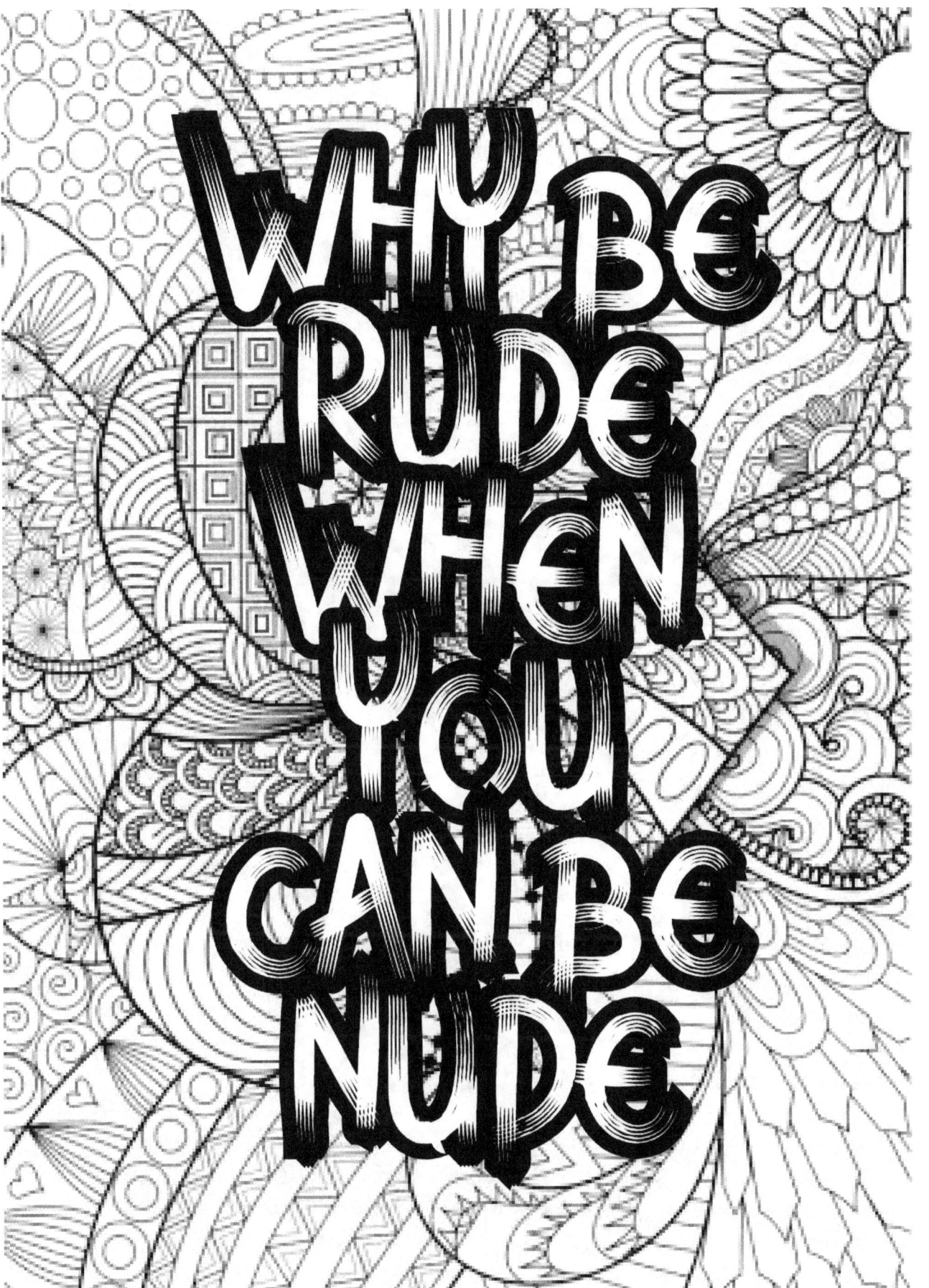

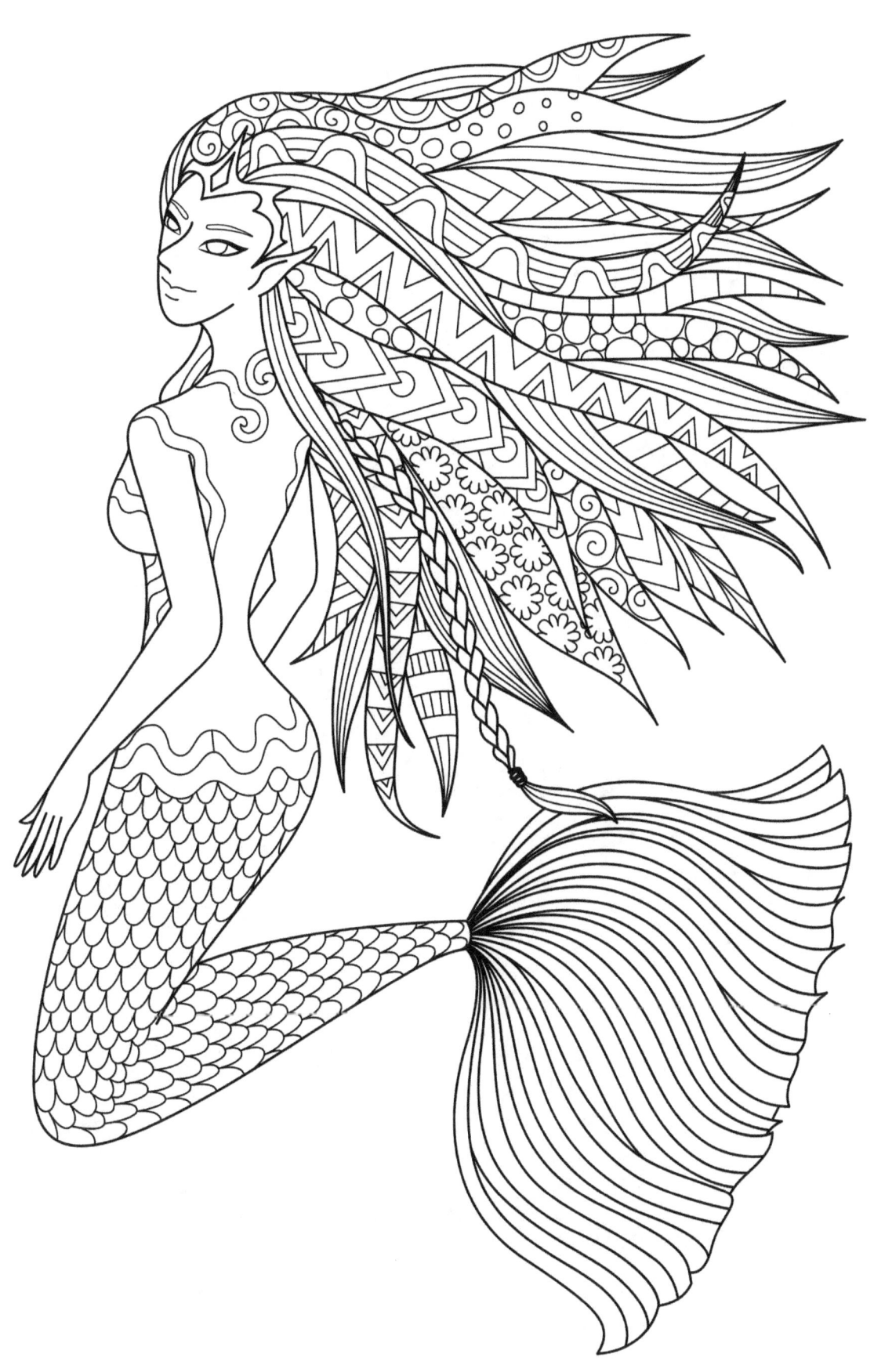

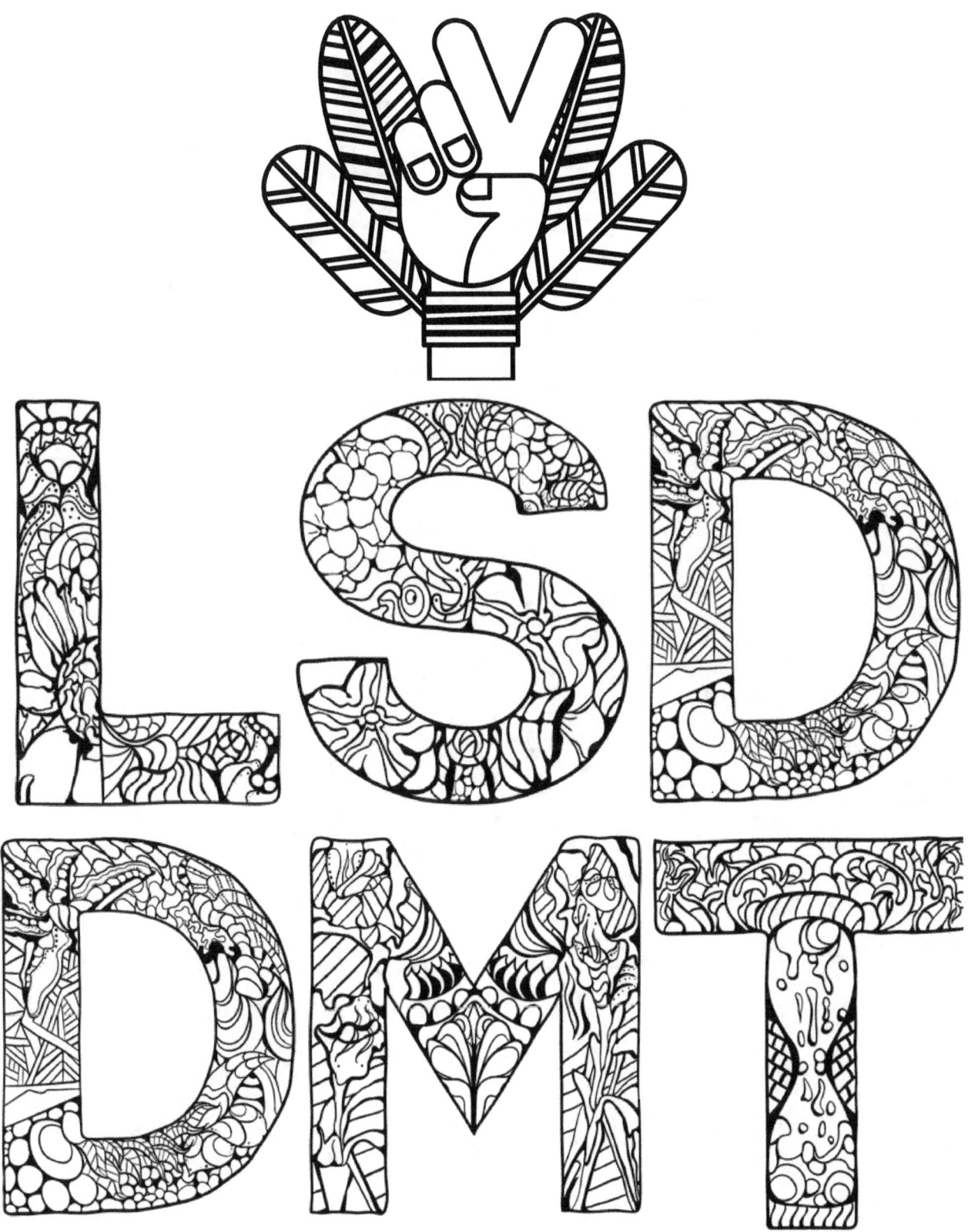

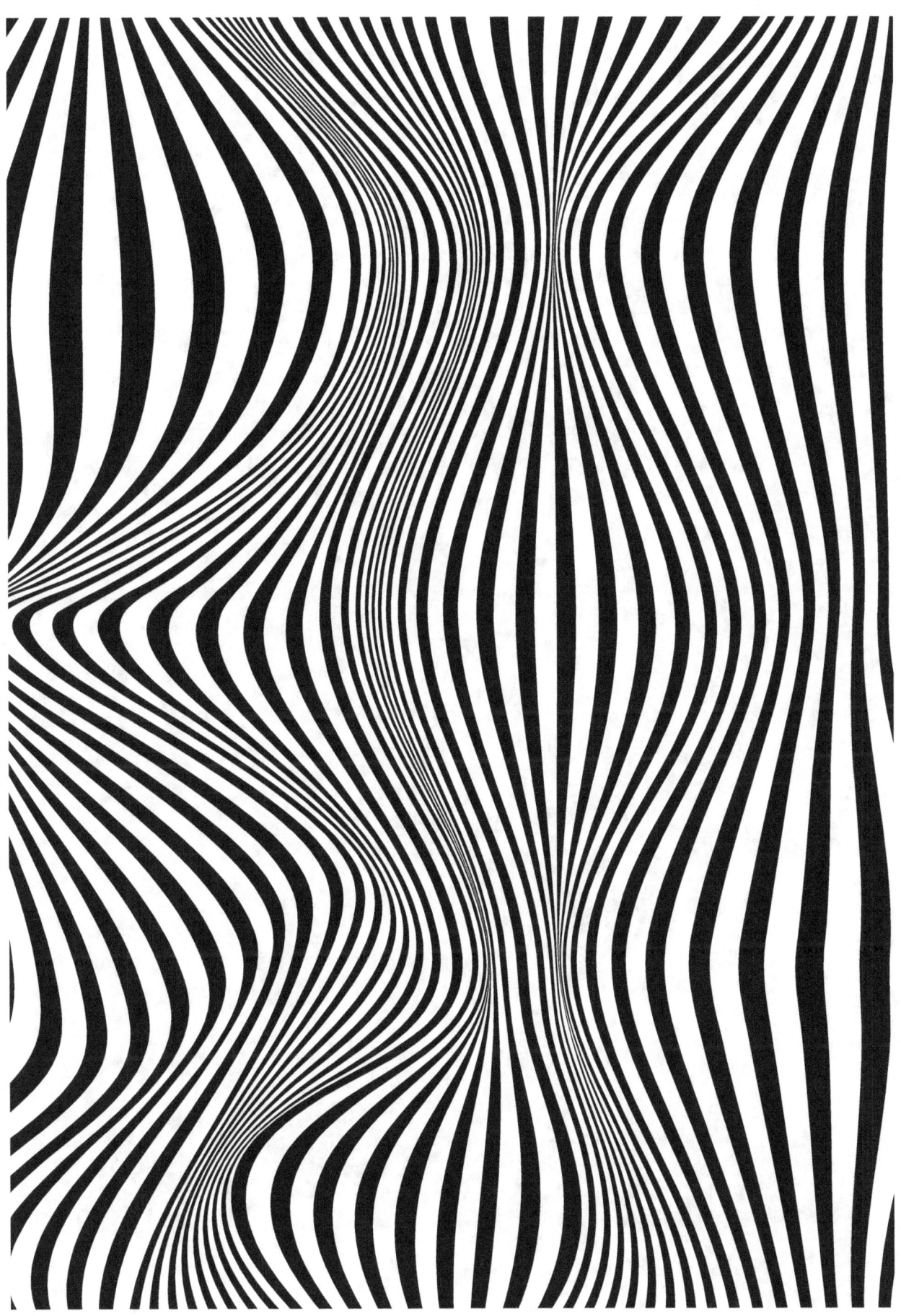

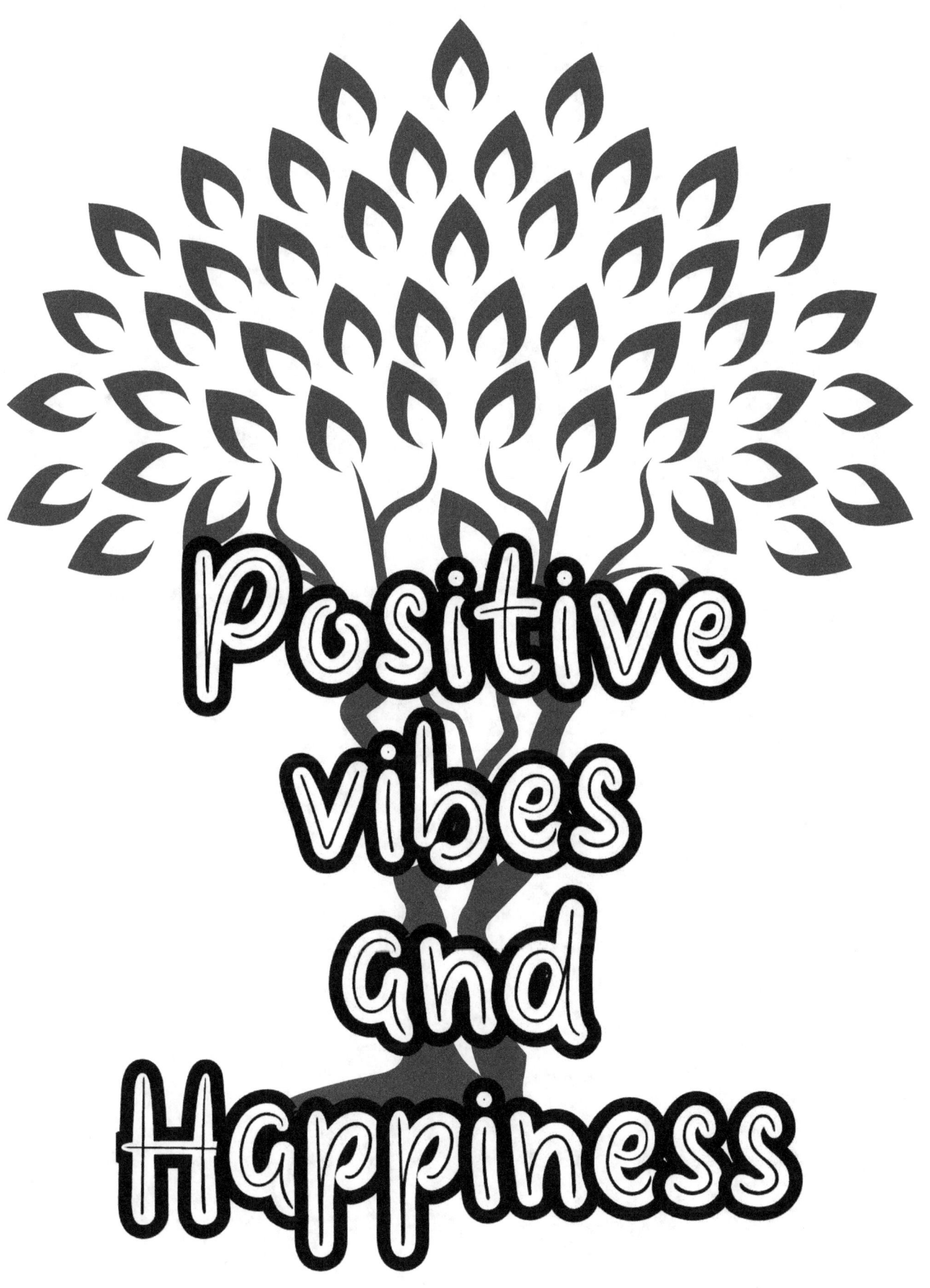

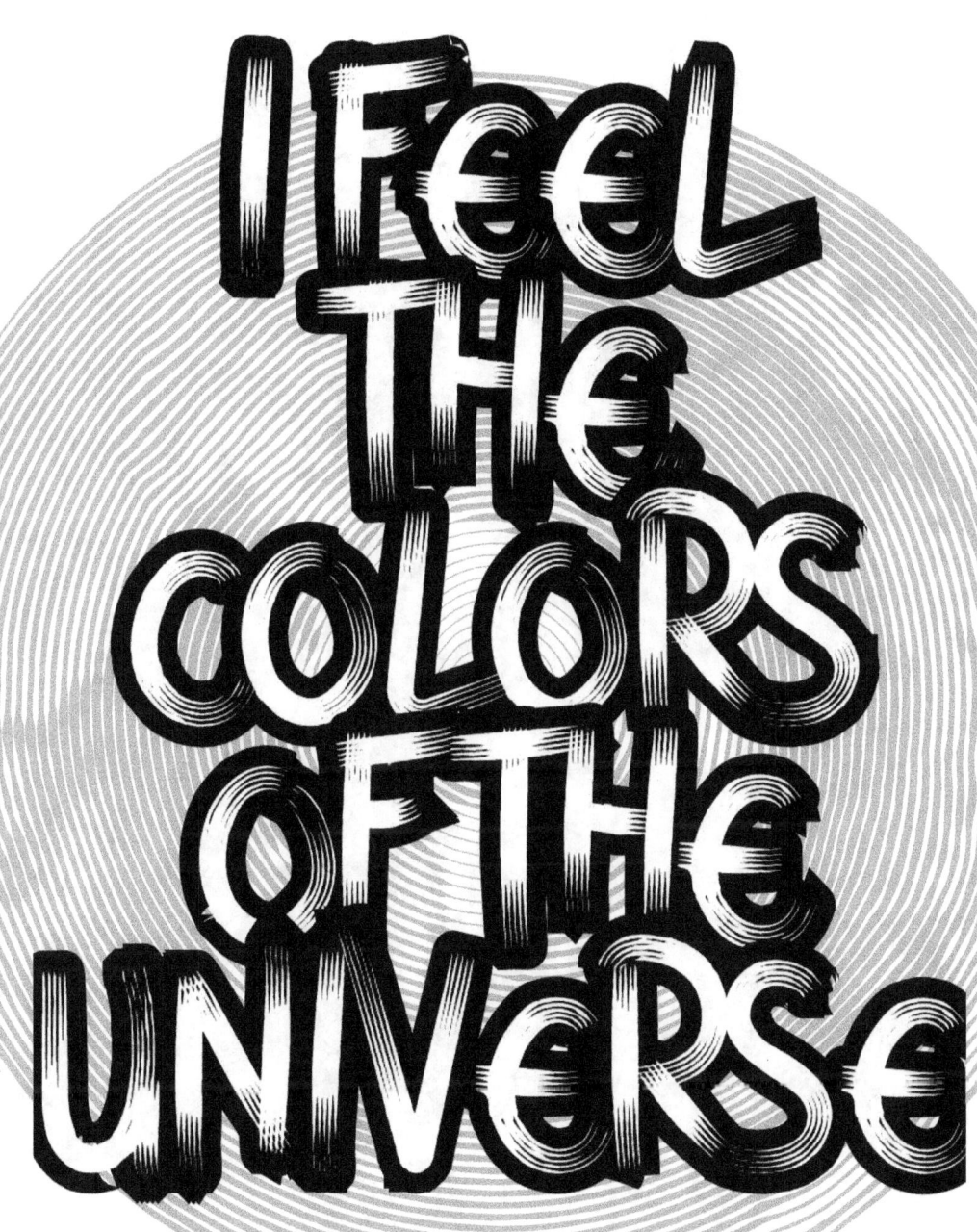

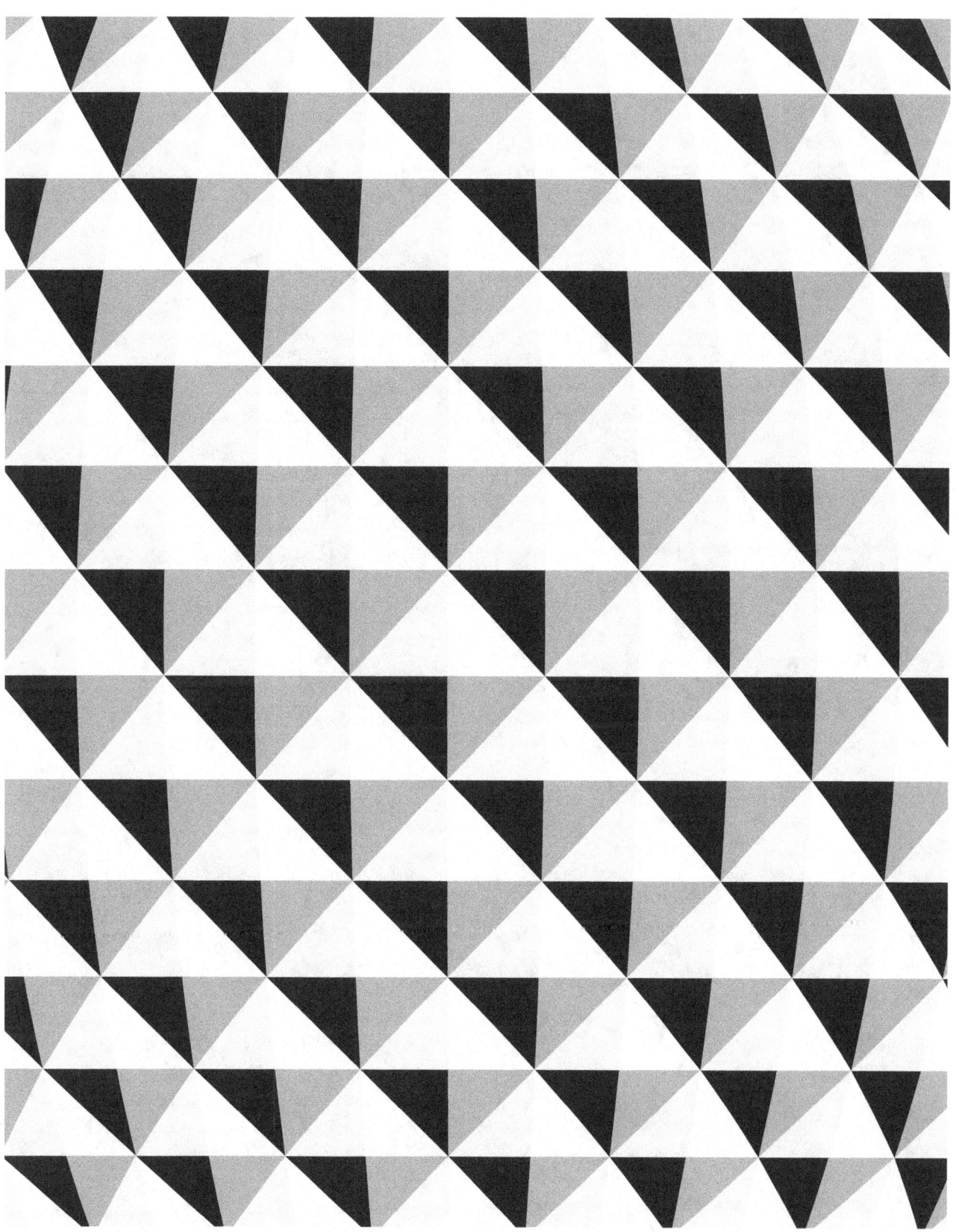

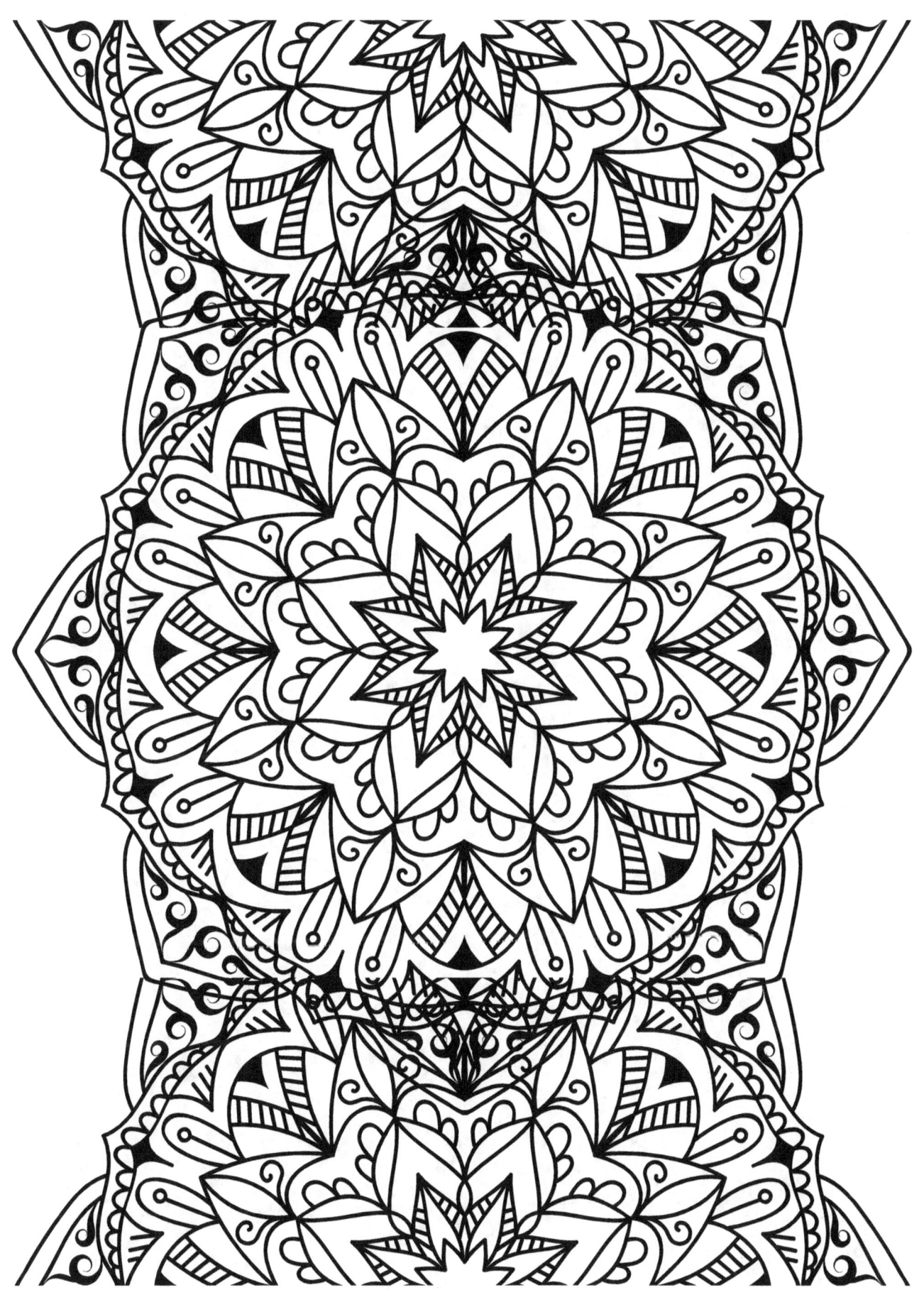

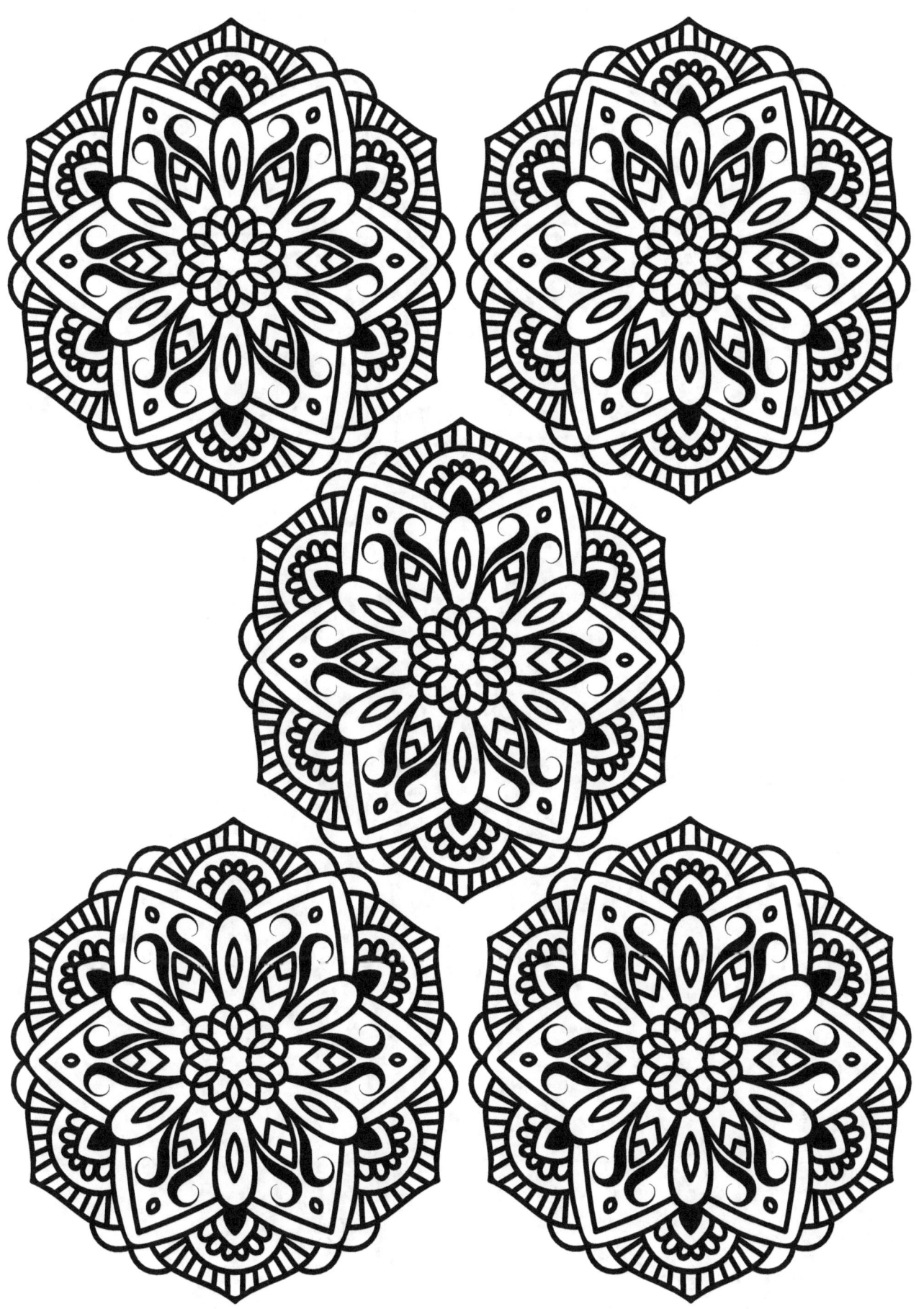

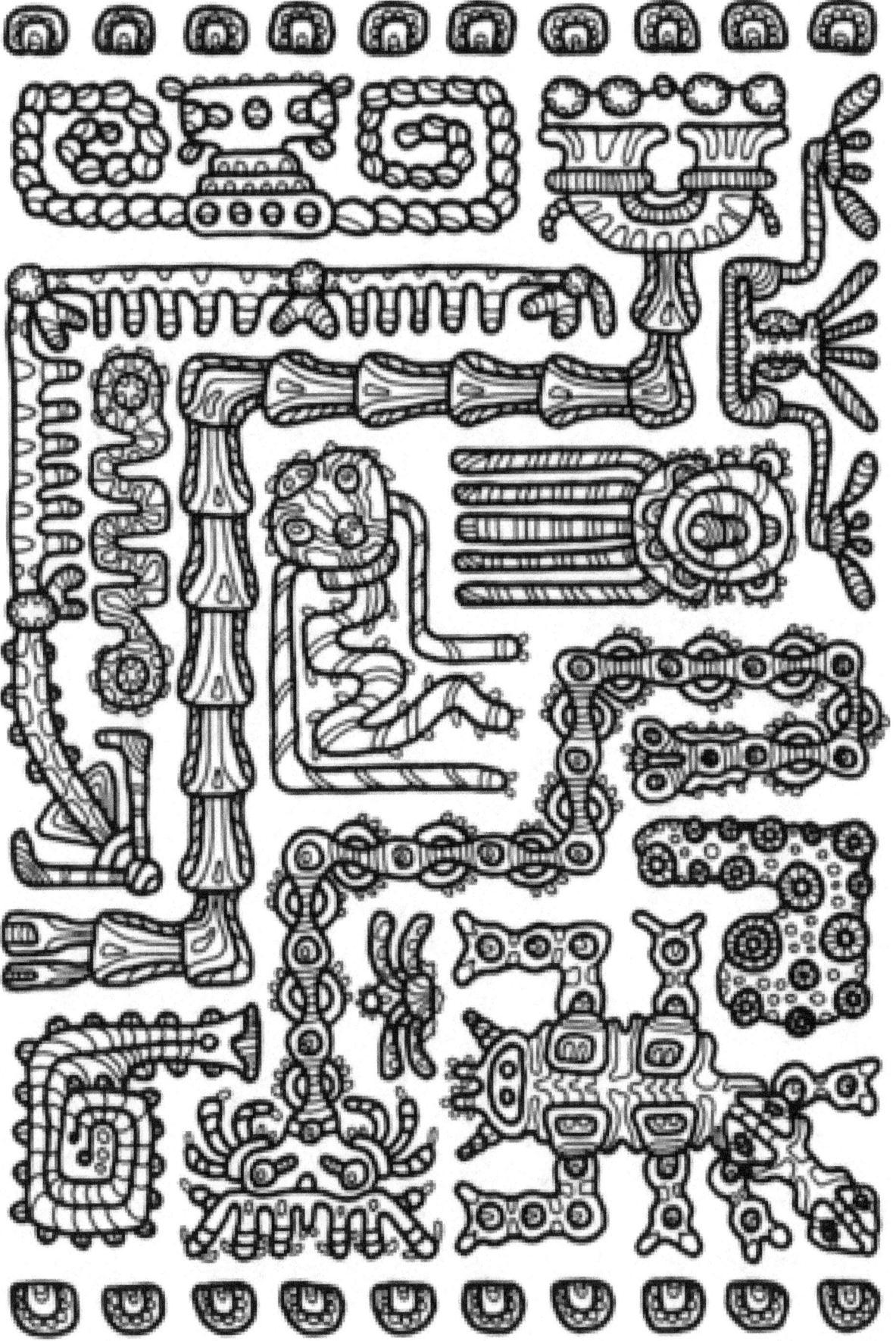

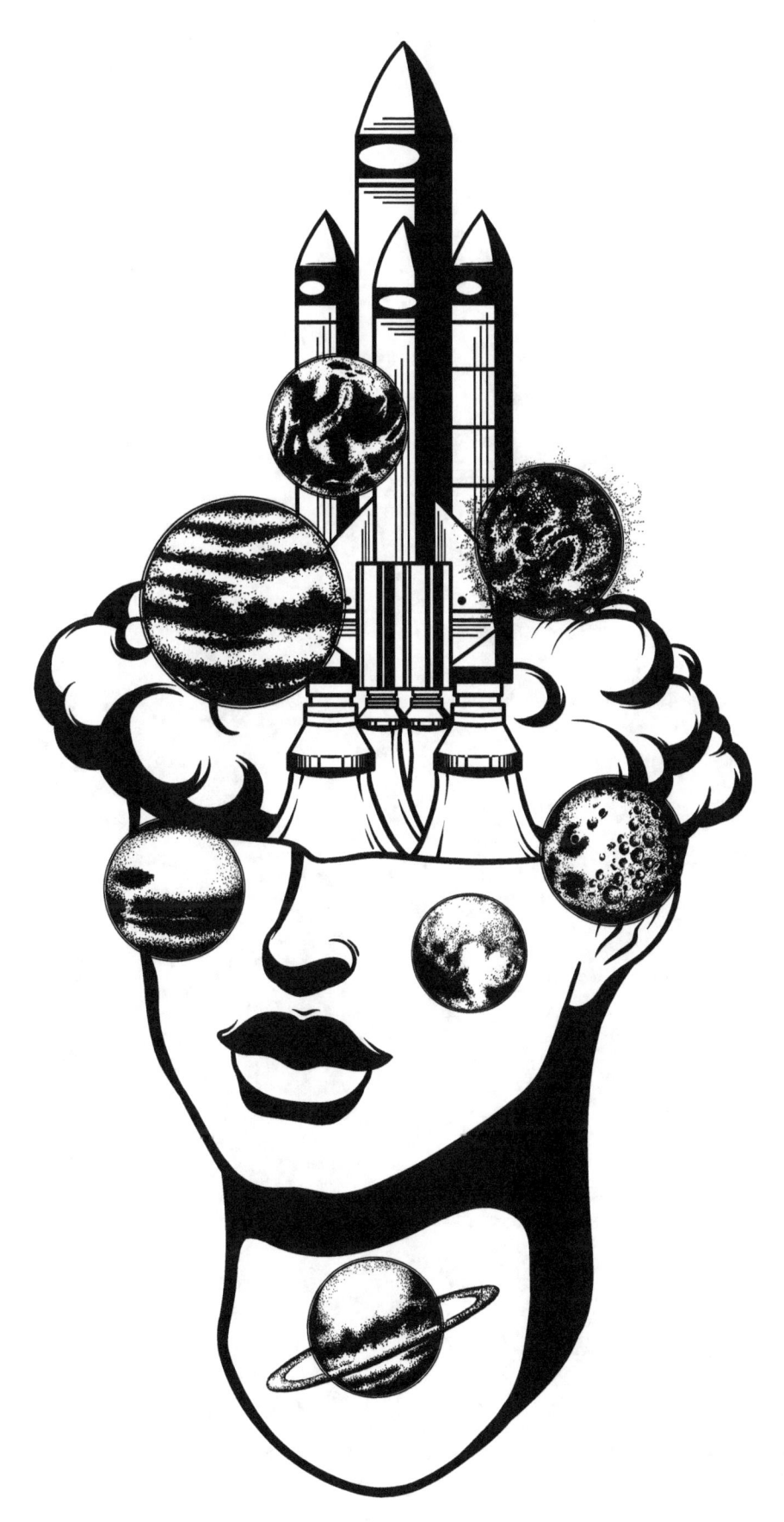

THE MORE YOU CARE THE MORE YOU LOOSE

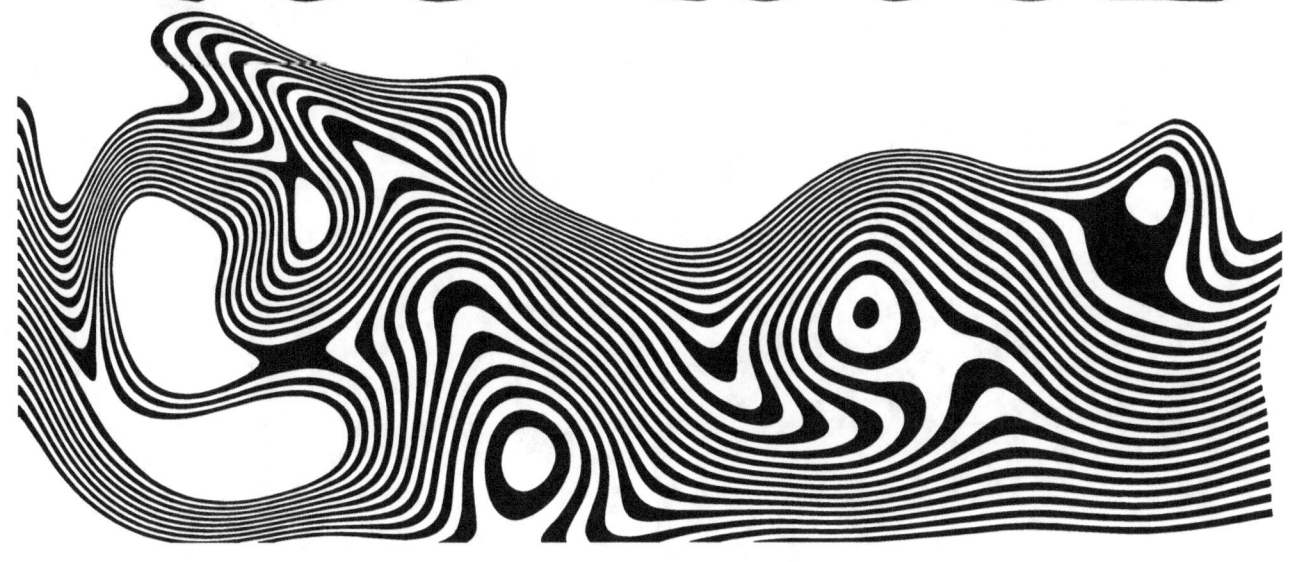

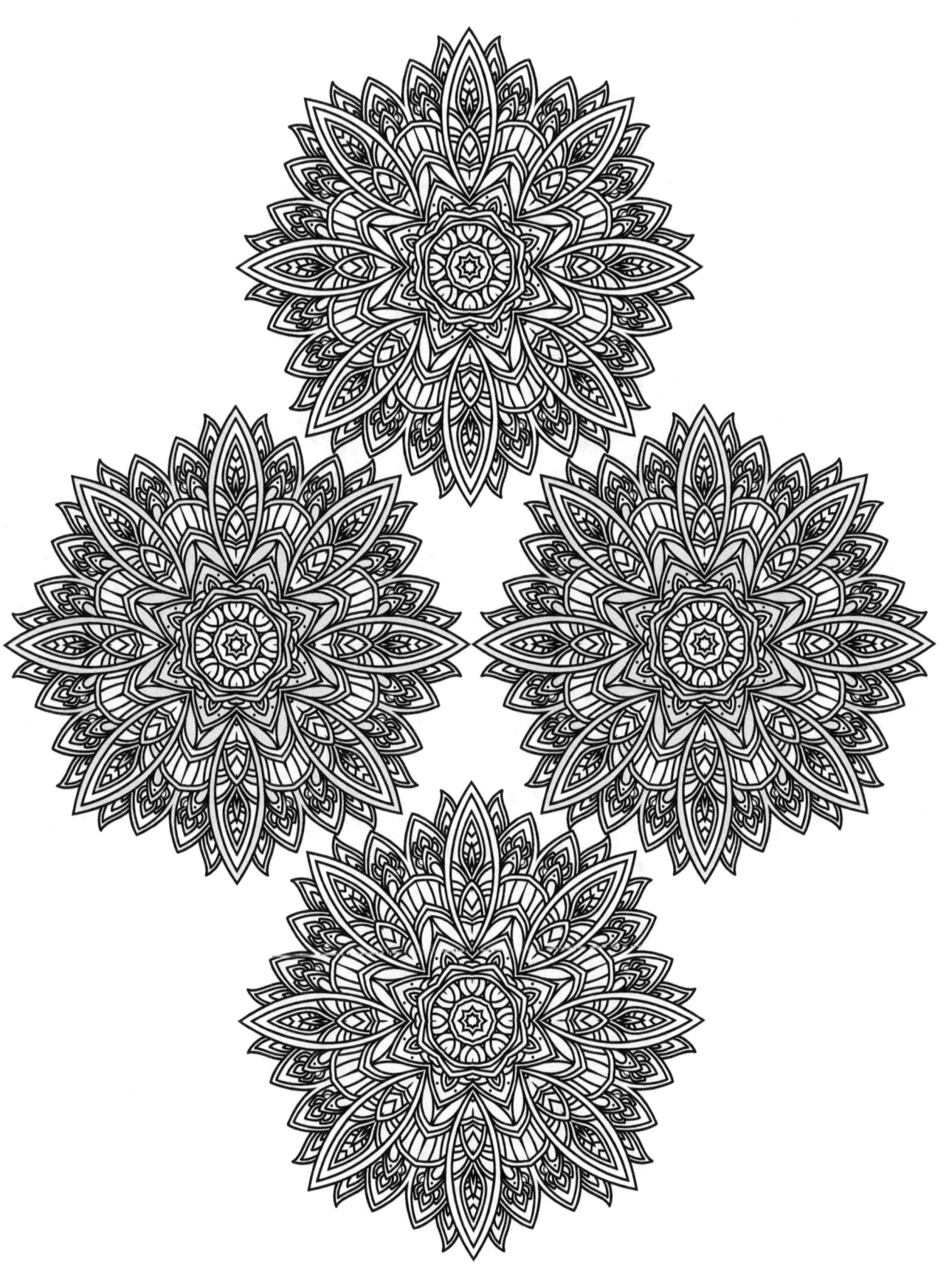

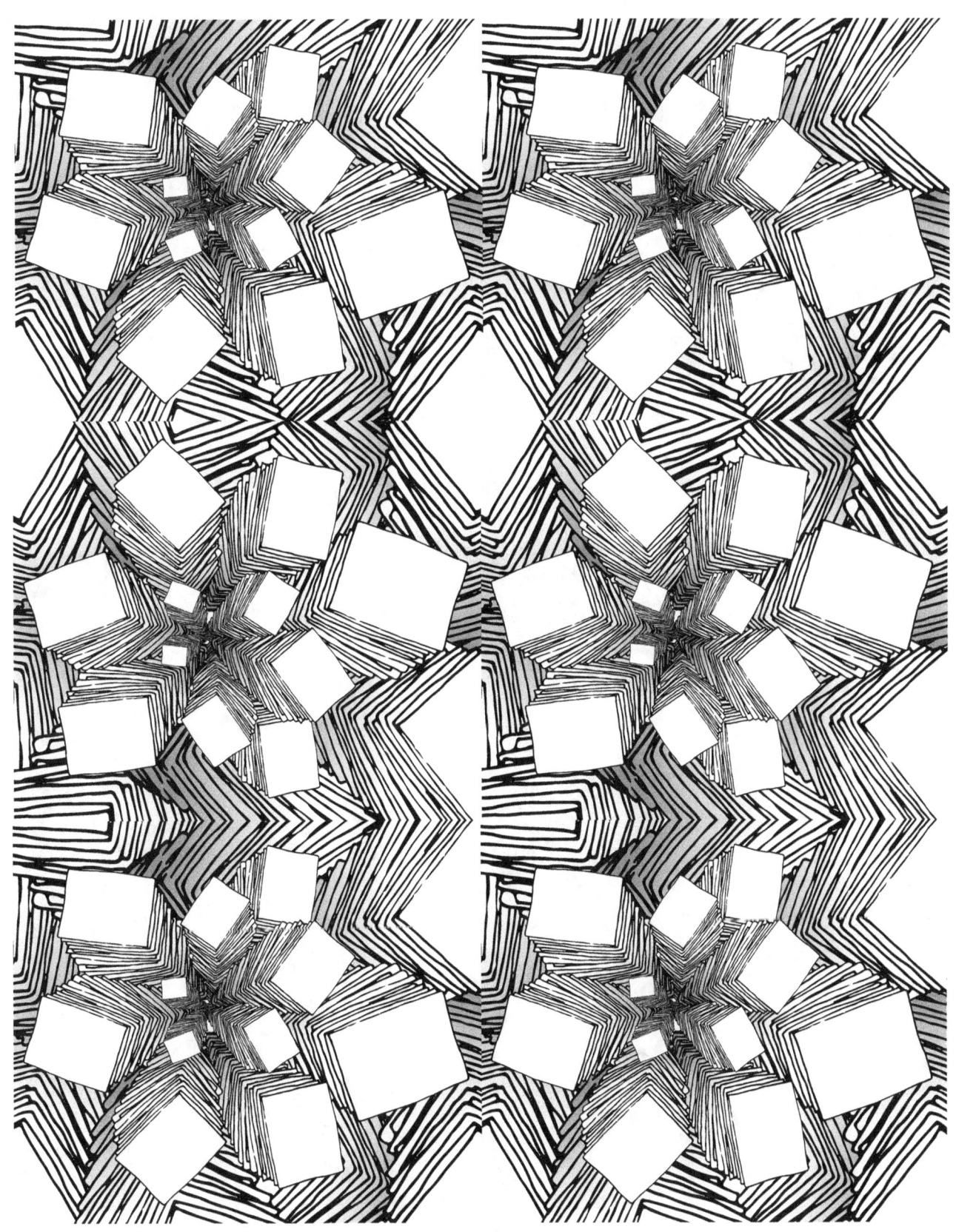

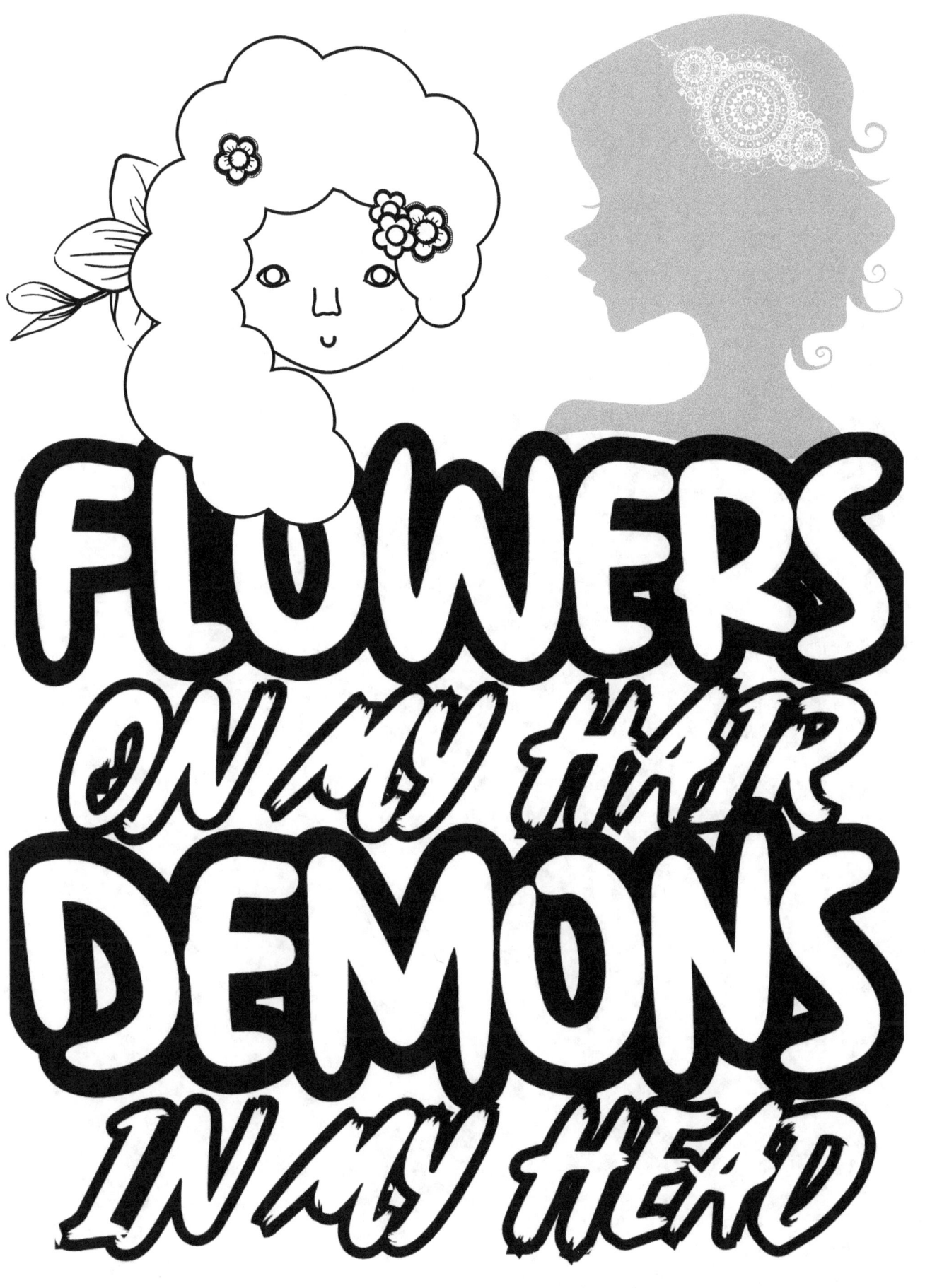

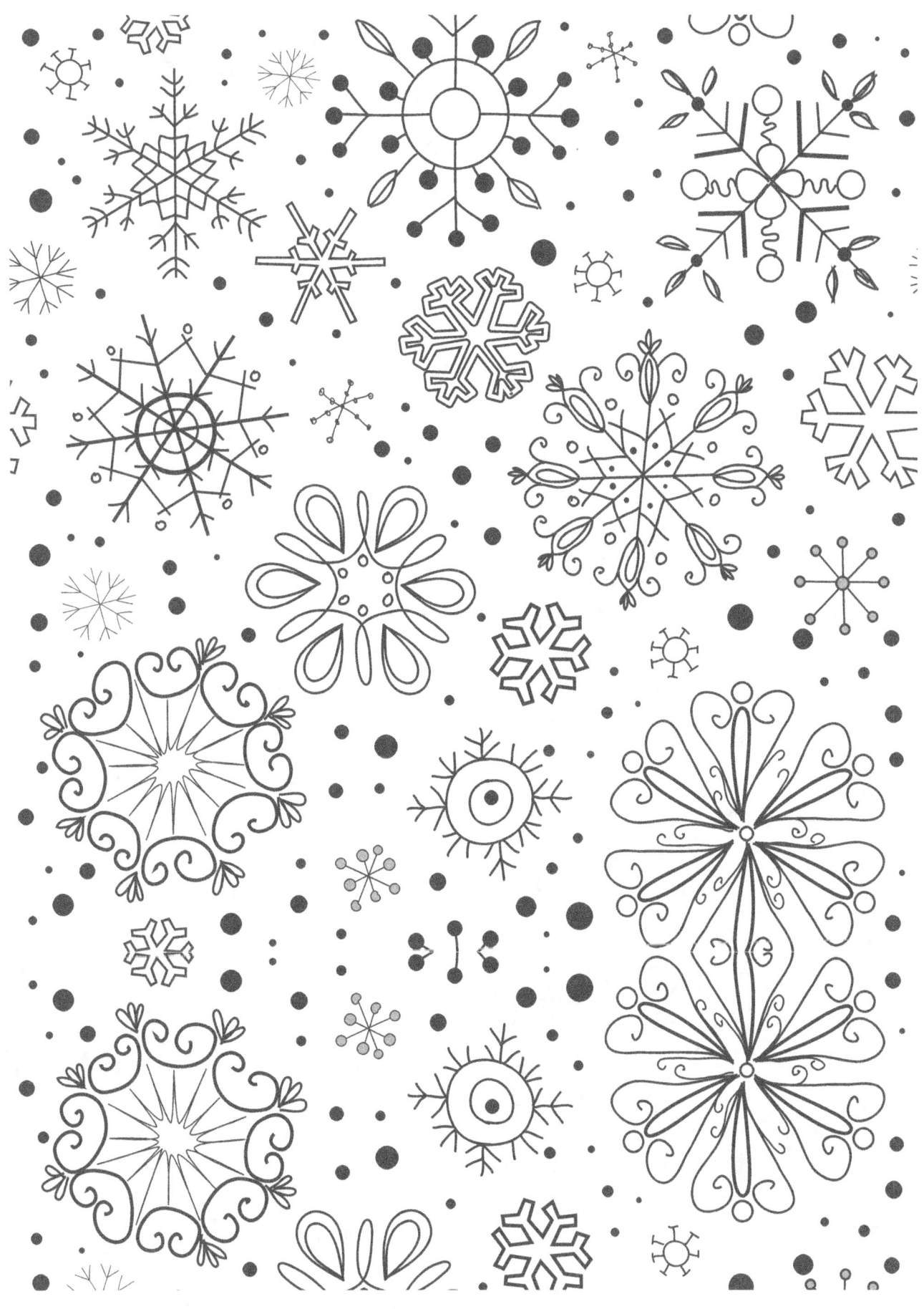

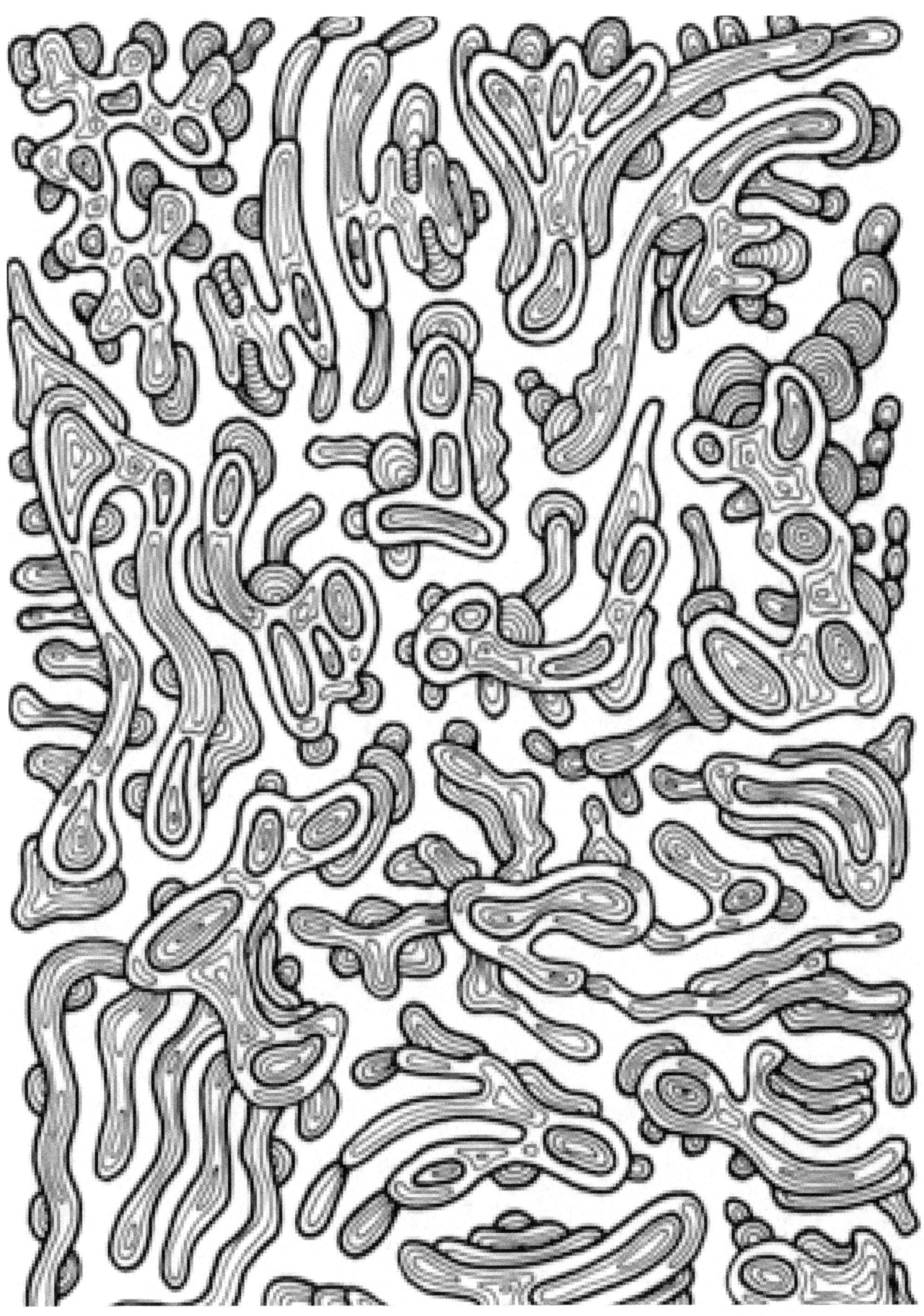

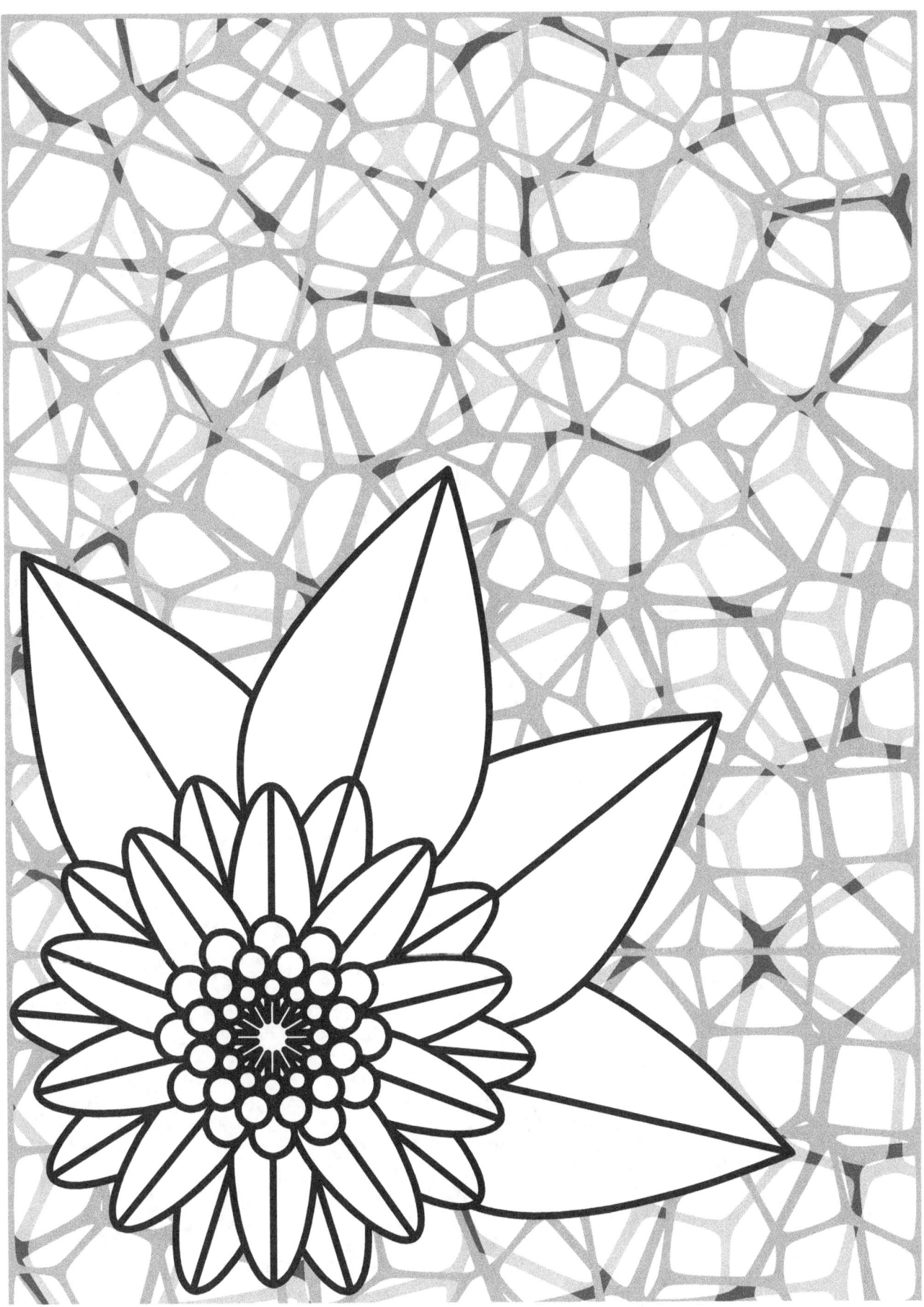

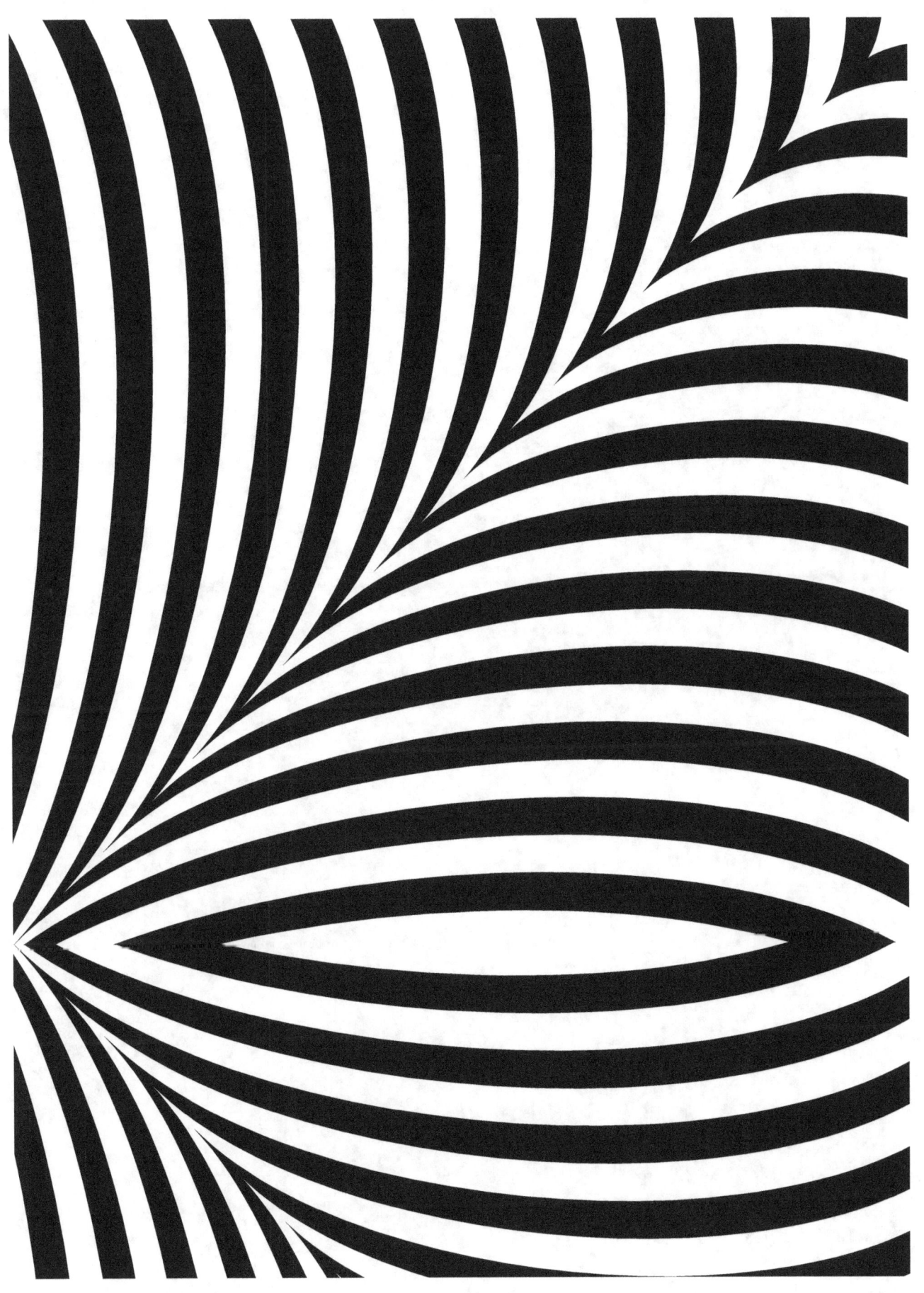

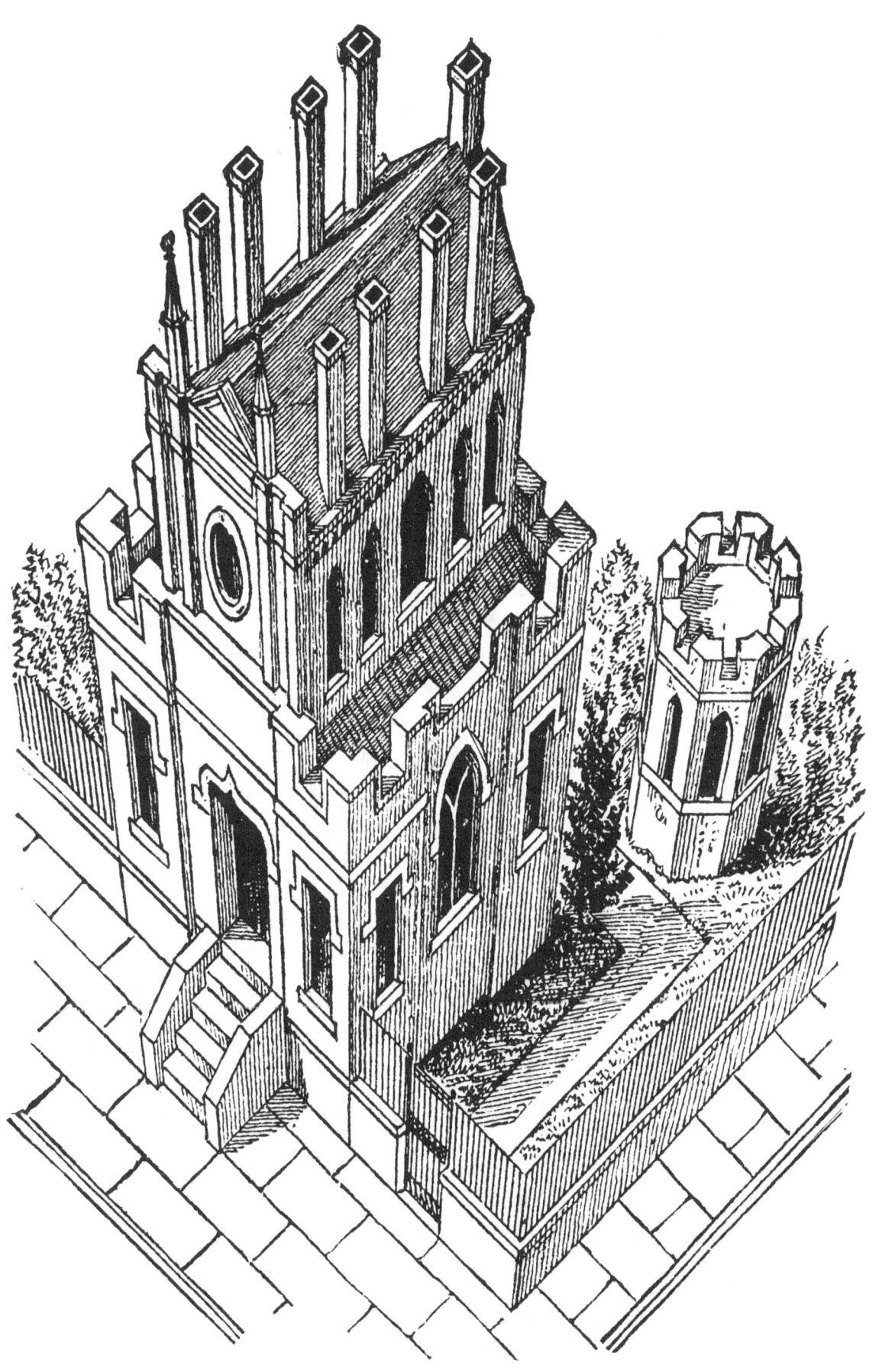

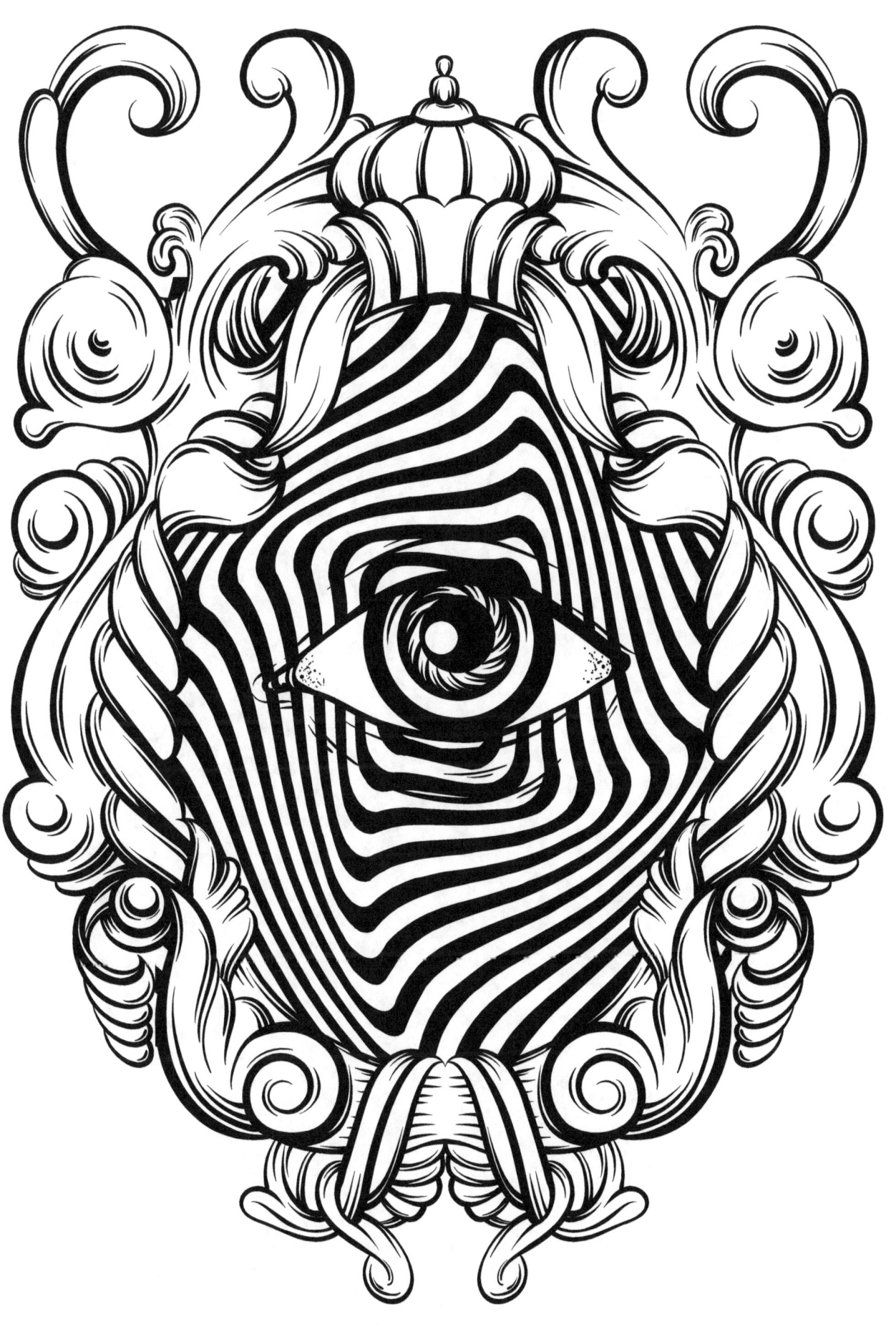

Think Free Live Free

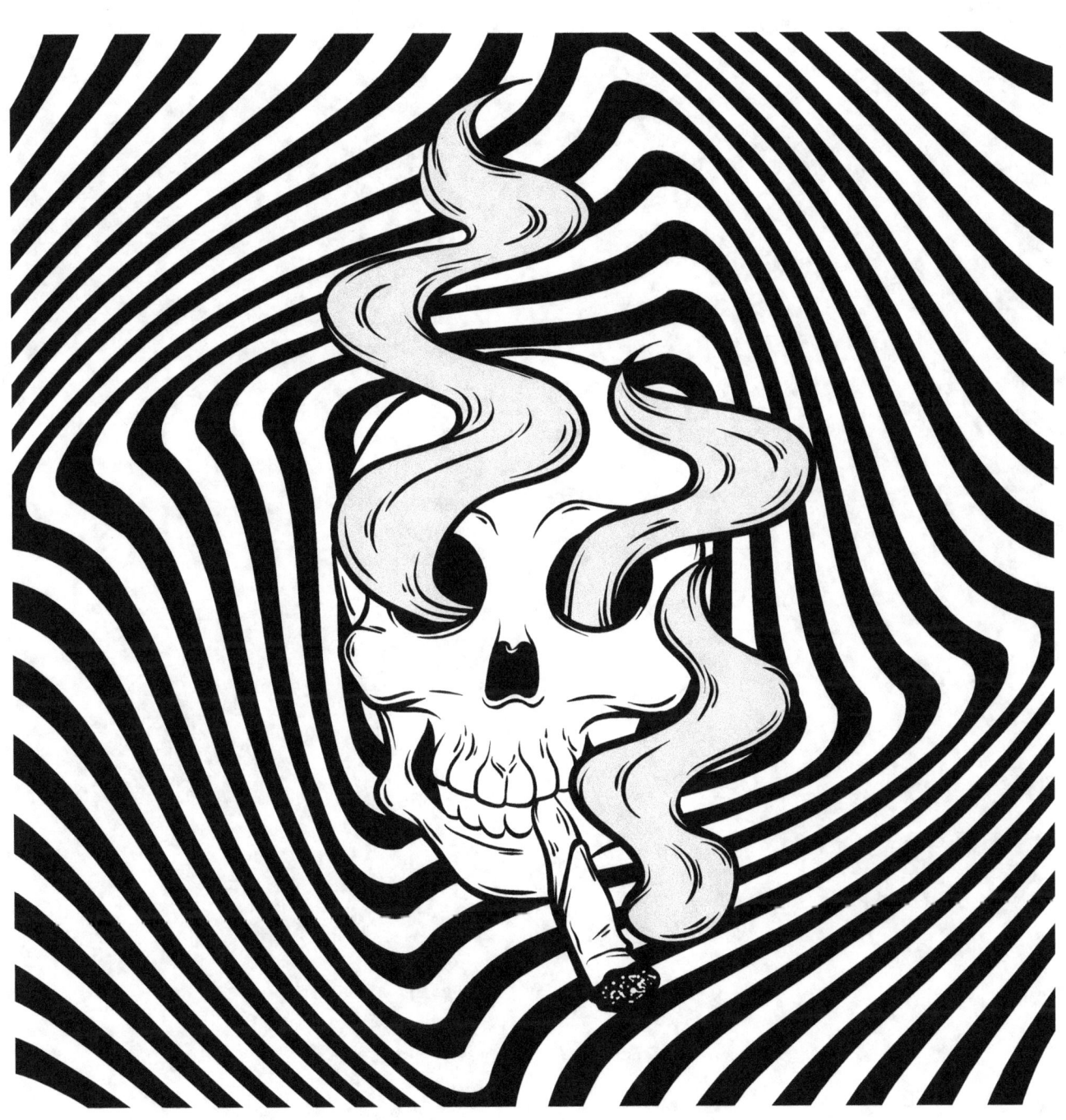

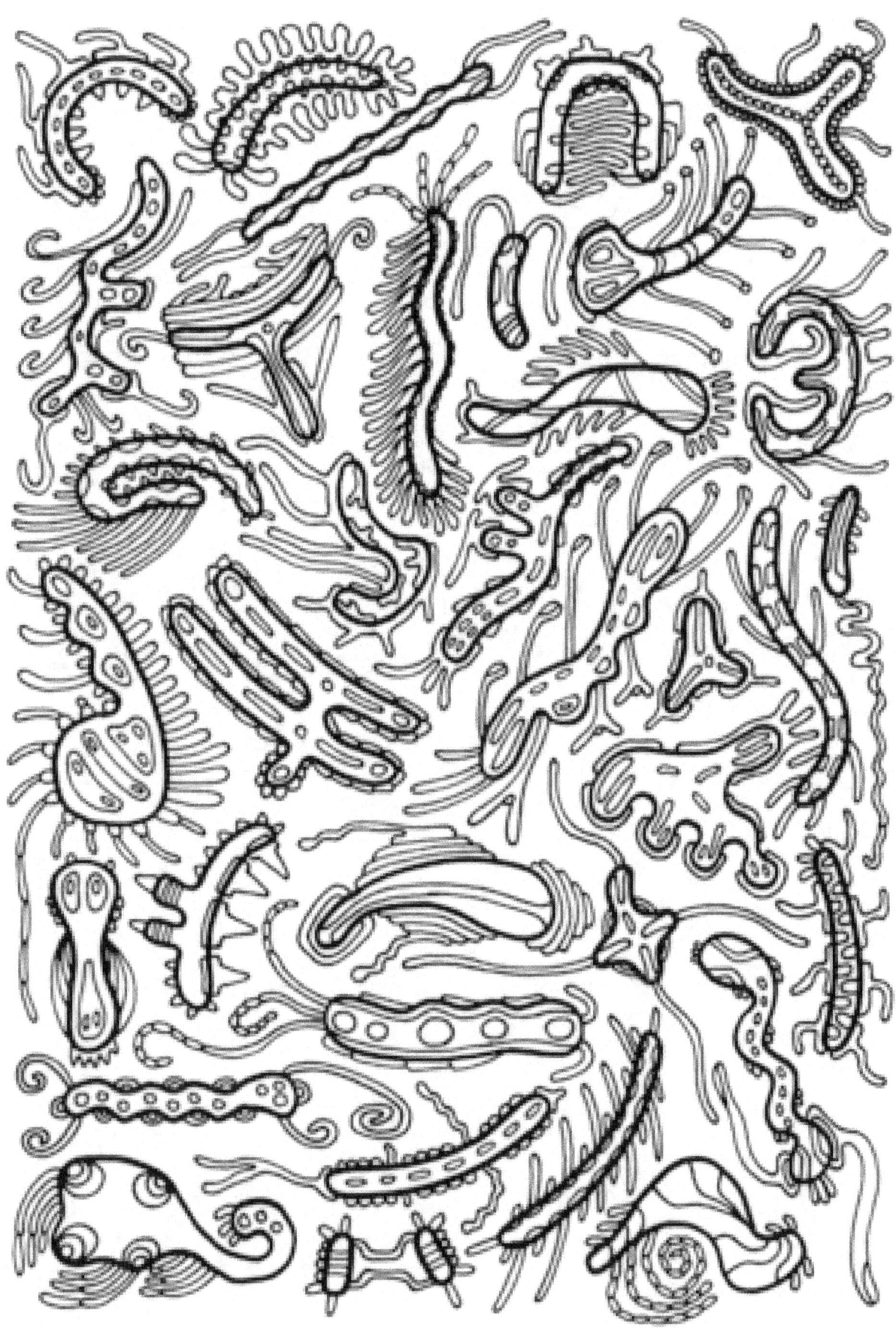

I believe in Acid

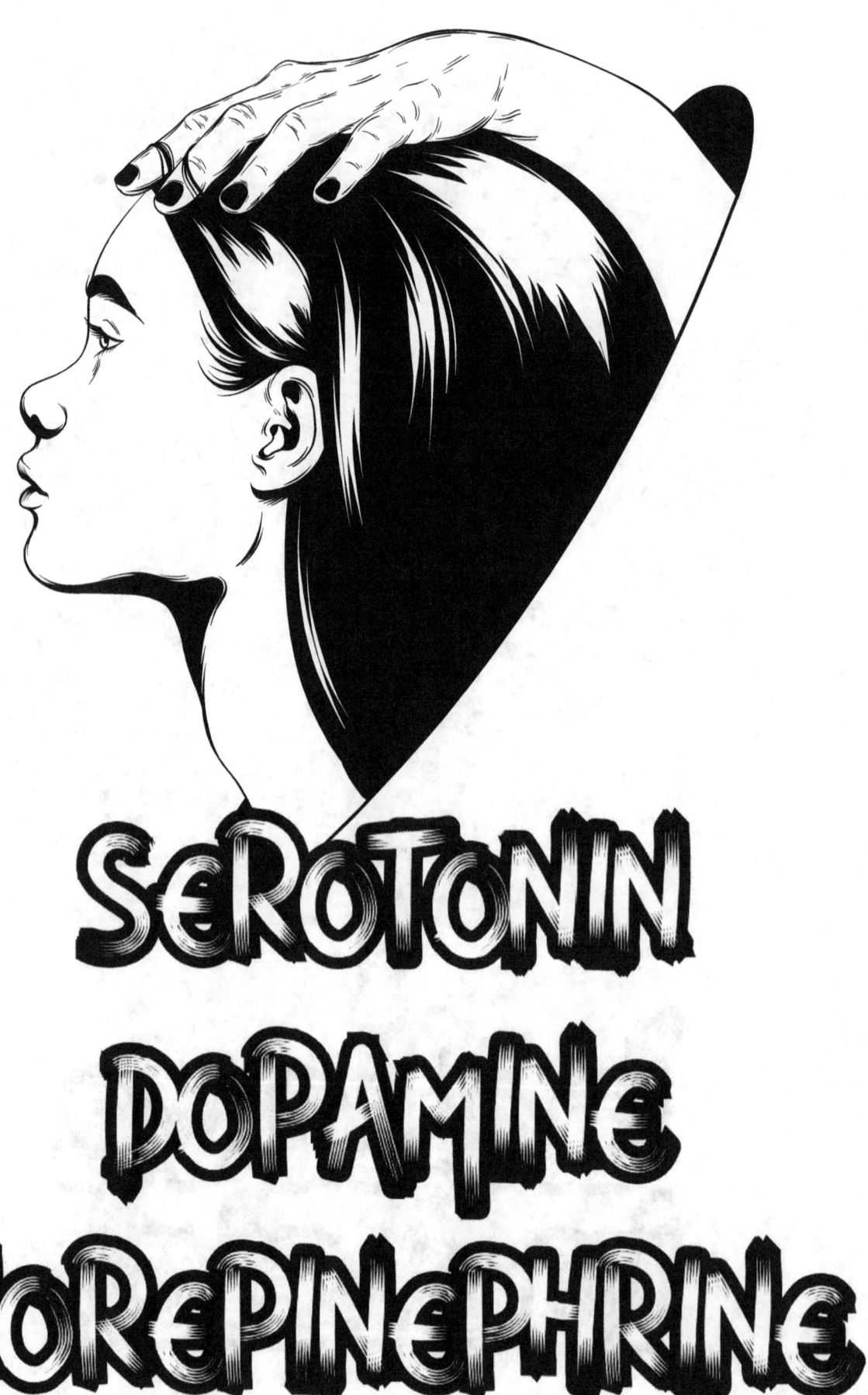

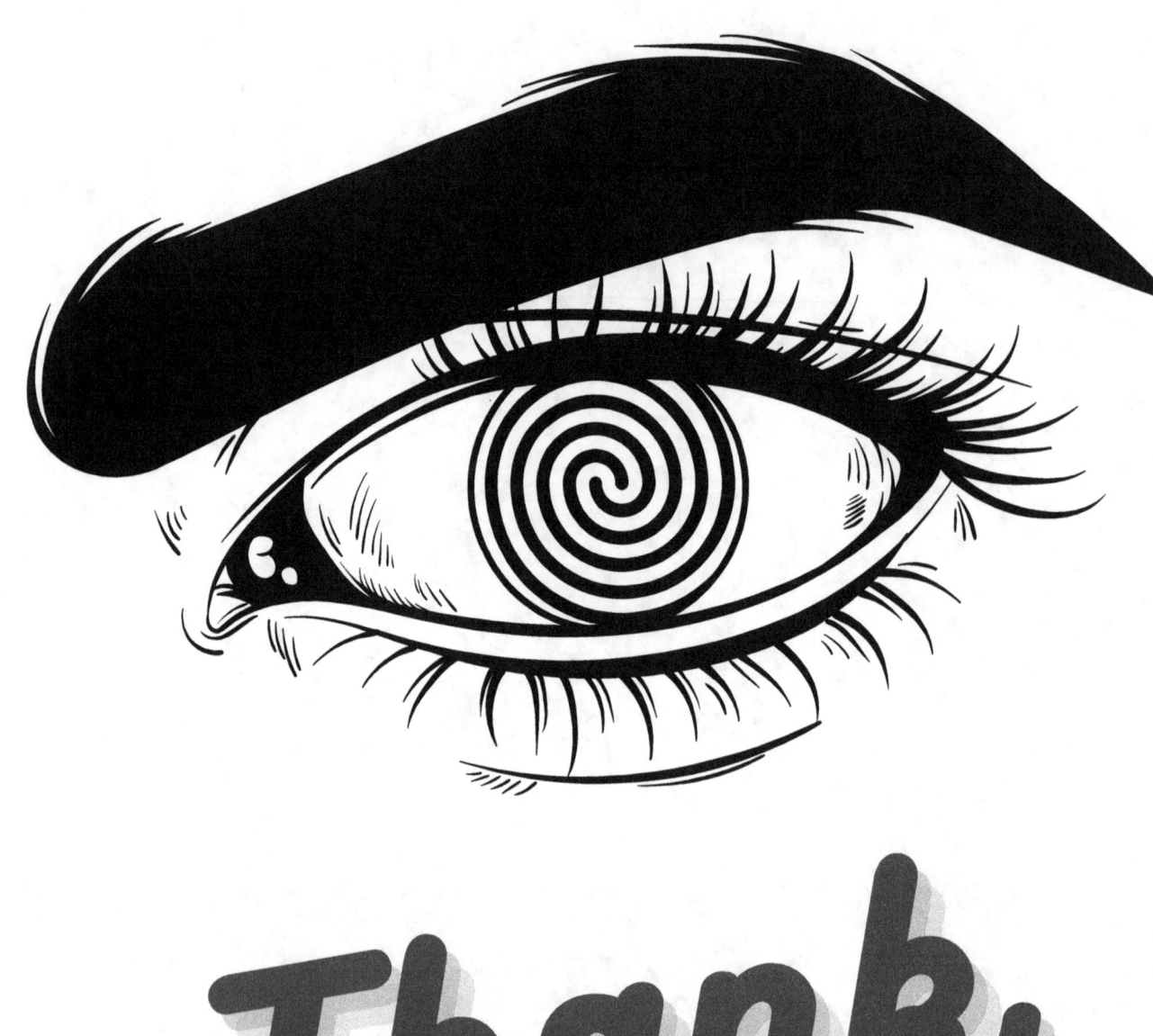

www.ingramcontent.com/pod-product-compliance
Lightning Source LLC
Chambersburg PA
CBHW080512220526

45465CB00006B/2451